HORSE TACK AND SADDLERY

HORSE TACK AND SADDLERY

THE COMPLETE ILLUSTRATED GUIDE TO RIDING EQUIPMENT

SARAH MUIR | PHOTOGRAPHY BY KIT HOUGHTON

LORENZ BOOKS

This edition is published by Lorenz Books, an imprint of Anness Publishing Ltd,

108 Great Russell Street, London WC1B 3NA; info@anness.com

www.lorenzbooks.com; www.annesspublishing.com; twitter: @Anness_Books

If you like the images in this book and would like to investigate using them for publishing, promotions
or advertising, please visit our website www.practicalpictures.com for more information.

© Anness Publishing Ltd 2016

A CIP catalogue record for this book is available from the British Library.

Publisher: Joanna Lorenz
Editor: Sarah Ainley
Copy Editor: Marion Paull
Designer: Michael Morey
Illustrator: Diane Breeze
Production Controller: Stephanie Moe

PUBLISHER'S NOTE

Contents

Introduction

The array of equipment available to the modern horse owner
is staggering. There is such a diverse range of bits that whole
books have been devoted to their usage; there are saddles of every
description; boots and bandages to protect all parts of the horse's
anatomy; rugs to keep him warm and dry; and an inexhaustible
supply of "gadgets" designed to control him.

For everyday riding purposes, however, a few items of
basic equipment will suffice: a saddle, a bridle and a few pieces
of horse clothing. The equipment should fit correctly if it is to be
effective, and only if it is well cared for will it prove hardwearing.
Saddlery and horse clothing should always be comfortable and
safe: riding is a high risk sport and no short cuts should be
taken in this respect.

▌ OPPOSITE
An impeccably ordered
tack room, with neatly
stored saddles and
bridles ready for use.

▌ LEFT
Horse tack can be
highly decorative as
well as practical.

The Saddle

The saddle is one of the most important pieces of equipment
for the ridden horse, and, because of the skill and craftsmanship
involved in producing a saddle, it is usually the most expensive.
The earliest type of saddle, first developed thousands of years
ago, was nothing more than a simple blanket kept in place with
breastplate and girth. The modern saddle, however, is a
sophisticated piece of equipment. It has evolved as a result of the
demands of modern equestrianism, whether it be the Western
saddle designed to withstand the rigours of cowboy life; the
dressage saddle designed to give the rider an elegant yet
effective position; or the minuscule racing saddle.
The saddle's design and fit can have a tremendous effect
on both the horse's performance and the rider's position.
An ill-fitting saddle can cause the horse considerable discomfort
and even physical damage. When choosing a new saddle,
therefore, it is always advisable to seek professional help –
a trained saddler will be able to ensure that the saddle
fits the horse correctly.

▮ OPPOSITE
The saddle is an
important and costly
piece of equipment,
and should always
be well cared for.

▮ LEFT
The Saddlebred saddle,
specially designed for
showing American
Saddlebreds and other
gaited horses.

Points of the Saddle

Virtually all saddles are built upon a solid framework called a tree. This framework was traditionally made from beech wood but is now available in laminated wood, and even fibreglass and plastic. It is the shape of the tree and the placing of the metal stirrup bars riveted to the tree which determine the size and shape of the saddle. The seat of the saddle is given shape by stretching a webbing and cotton fabric over the tree. Serge or a synthetic fabric is stretched to form the seat shape and a wool or synthetic stuffing provides the padding below.

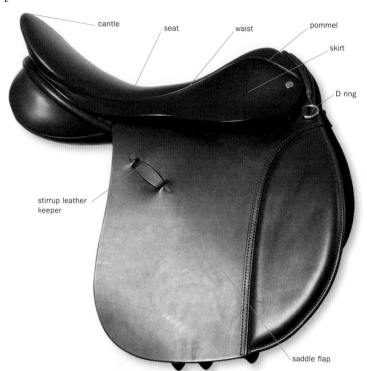

cantle • seat • waist • pommel • skirt • D ring • stirrup leather keeper • saddle flap

■ ABOVE
The general purpose saddle is the standard model for the sport. The moderate features make it suitable for all riding disciplines at a non-professional level. Specialist saddles develop individual characteristics of the general purpose saddle according to the needs of the particular discipline.

■ RIGHT
Under the saddle flap. Most saddles have three girth straps. The first two are fixed to the web strap attached to the tree and the third is fixed independently.

point of tree • knee roll • buckle guard • sweat flap • girth straps (billets) • saddle flap

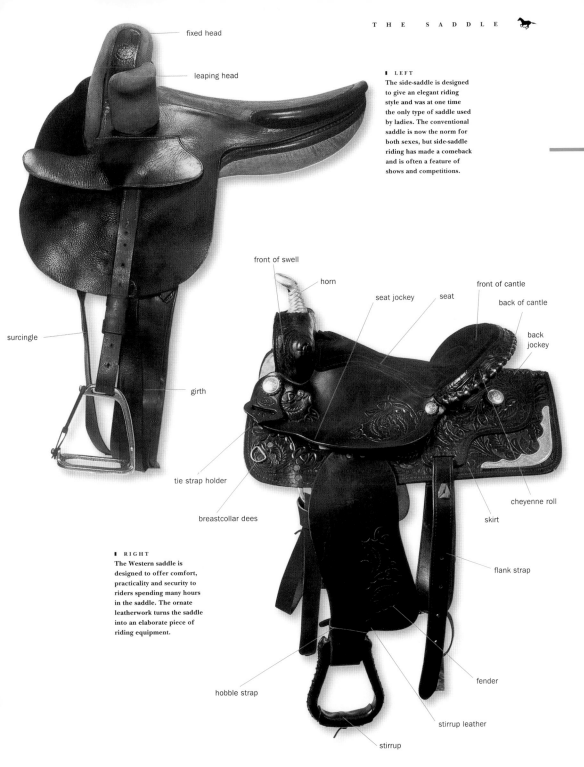

fixed head

leaping head

front of swell

horn

seat jockey

seat

front of cantle

back of cantle

back
jockey

surcingle

girth

tie strap holder

breastcollar dees

cheyenne roll

skirt

flank strap

fender

hobble strap

stirrup leather

stirrup

Riding and Competing Saddles

Saddles are available in a number of shapes and styles to suit the many equestrian disciplines at every level of competition from novice to professional.

The **leather general purpose (GP) saddle** is designed to be used across the board of riding activities. It is ideal for pleasure riding, hunting, novice cross-country and show jumping and basic dressage. A less expensive alternative to the leather saddle is the **synthetic general purpose saddle**, which is lighter in weight than the leather type, and easier to clean.

For most riders, the general purpose saddle is perfectly adequate for jumping. However, if you are riding at a competitive level and tackling larger fences, you may prefer the specialist design of the jumping saddle. The saddle flaps of the **Crosby close-contact jumping saddle** are more forward cut than those of the general purpose saddle. This enables you to keep your legs close to the saddle even when riding with a short stirrup length.

The **event saddle** is very similar in style to a general purpose saddle and can be used for all phases of horse trials, although some riders prefer to have an additional saddle for the dressage phase. Many famous riders have become involved in the design of saddles and the event saddle illustrated was developed by the international eventer, Mary King.

The **Albion Selecta** is a multi-purpose saddle which aims to combine the general purpose saddle with a dressage and a jumping saddle. It features easily removable knee pads which allow the saddle to be adapted for all riding disciplines from pleasure riding to jumping, dressage, cross-country and working hunter events.

The **polo saddle** has a relatively flat seat, extra-long sweat flaps and no knee and thigh rolls. It is designed specifically for the game of polo, during which the horse travels at speed and the rider needs to be able to move with ease to hit the ball.

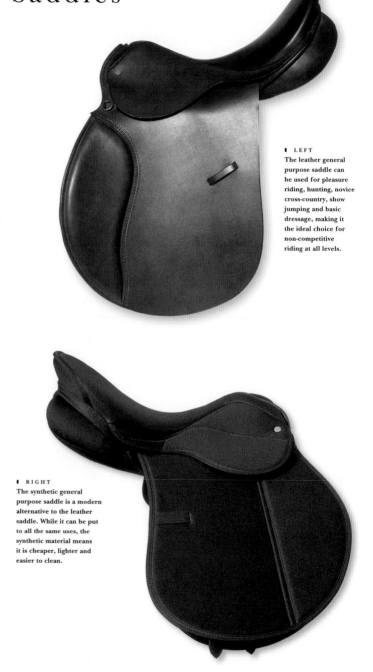

■ LEFT
The leather general purpose saddle can be used for pleasure riding, hunting, novice cross-country, show jumping and basic dressage, making it the ideal choice for non-competitive riding at all levels.

■ RIGHT
The synthetic general purpose saddle is a modern alternative to the leather saddle. While it can be put to all the same uses, the synthetic material means it is cheaper, lighter and easier to clean.

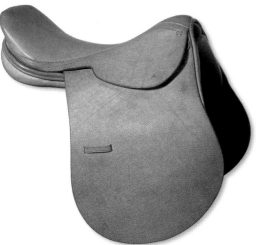

ABOVE
The polo saddle has a flat seat, extended sweat flaps and no knee or thigh rolls, all of which allow the rider freedom of movement when striking the ball.

BELOW LEFT
Event saddle. This is similar in style to the general purpose saddle and can be used for all phases of horse trials.

RIGHT
The Crosby close-contact jumping saddle. The saddle flaps are more forward cut than those of the general purpose saddle. This allows the rider to carry his legs closer to the saddle, and makes his position more secure.

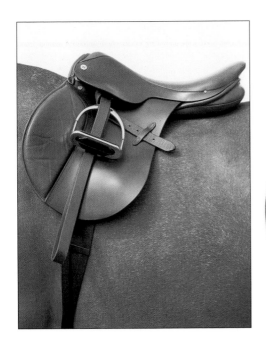

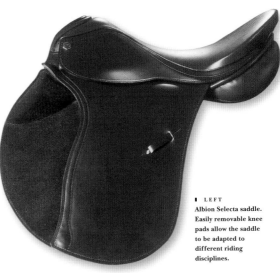

LEFT
Albion Selecta saddle. Easily removable knee pads allow the saddle to be adapted to different riding disciplines.

Showing Saddles

There are a number of saddles designed specifically to improve the horse's performance in showing competitions.

The purpose of the **showing saddle** is primarily to enhance the appearance of the show horse rather than to increase the comfort of the rider. The saddle is straight cut to show off the horse's shoulder and is simple in design, since it is the horse rather than the tack that is being judged. The showing saddle is a specialized piece of equipment and not always very comfortable; many riders prefer to use a dressage saddle for showing classes.

The **dressage saddle**, designed for riding and schooling horses on the flat rather than over jumps, has longer and straighter flaps than the general purpose saddle. This allows you to carry your legs in a longer position and closer to the horse's body. To eliminate bulk under your legs, longer girth straps (billets) are fitted and used with a short dressage girth.

The **Saddlebred saddle** is for showing American Saddlebreds and other gaited horses. It features a cut-back pommel (called a "cow-mouth") and very wide saddle flaps, which enable the rider to sit much further back in the saddle than usual.

For showing classes in which the horse is required both to jump and to be ridden on the flat, the **working hunter saddle** is ideal. The seat is deeper than the showing saddle, and padded knee rolls give a more secure seat which is helpful when jumping.

The **side-saddle,** first developed for ladies in the fourteenth century, allows the rider to carry both legs on the near (left) side of the horse, with the left foot in a stirrup and the right leg hooked over the pommel. The flat seat has a suede or doeskin cover for extra grip. Although no longer in general use, shows often feature ladies' hunter classes for side-saddle riders.

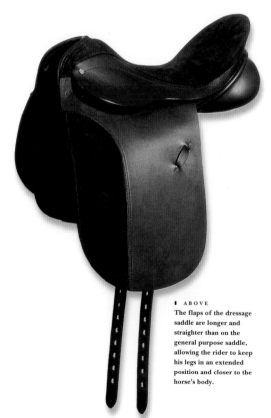

▌ ABOVE
The flaps of the dressage saddle are longer and straighter than on the general purpose saddle, allowing the rider to keep his legs in an extended position and closer to the horse's body.

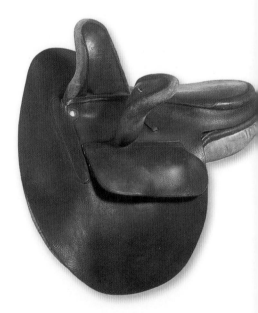

▌ ABOVE
The shape of the side-saddle allows the rider to adopt a more elegant position, with both legs on the near (left) side of the horse.

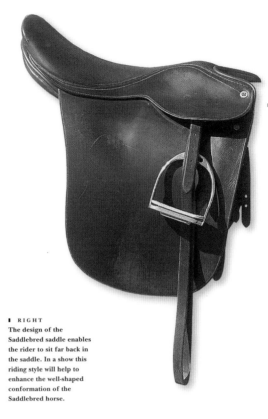

■ ABOVE
This showing saddle in
split hide, designed by
producer and rider Lynn
Russell, is specially shaped
to suit larger show horses
such as cobs and hunters.

■ RIGHT
The design of the
Saddlebred saddle enables
the rider to sit far back in
the saddle. In a show this
riding style will help to
enhance the well-shaped
conformation of the
Saddlebred horse.

■ RIGHT
The working hunter saddle
is a compromise between a
showing saddle and a
jumping saddle.

Trail-riding and Working Saddles

Saddles which are to be ridden over long periods of time need to have an element of comfort incorporated into the design.

The **endurance saddle**, as its name suggests, is designed for long-distance rides. The seat has extra padding and the saddle panels have extra width, thereby spreading the rider's weight over a greater area and reducing the risk of localized pressure points on the horse's back. Additional D rings are fitted to the saddle so that equipment, such as lead ropes and sponges, can easily be accommodated.

The **Australian stock saddle** is a utilitarian saddle designed for the comfort of both horse and rider during the hours spent driving cattle. The weight distribution properties mean that modified versions of this saddle can also be used for endurance or trail-riding.

The **Western reining saddle** is higher in front than the standard Western saddle, preventing the rider from being thrown forward when the horse performs the characteristic sliding stop. **Western pleasure saddles** are lighter in weight than working saddles and have only one cinch attachment. Comfortable and secure, these saddles are ideal for long-distance or trail-riding.

The **parade saddle** is an ornate working saddle featuring highly intricate metal and leatherwork. These decorative saddles are specially designed for use in carnival or rodeo parades.

The **trooper** or **Cavalry saddle** is built around a steel and wood tree and is the traditional choice of the armed forces because of its strength and durability.

The **military fan saddle** is designed for working horses, such as those used by the mounted police. The saddle tree distributes the rider's weight evenly for comfort during long periods of work, often when the horse is stationary.

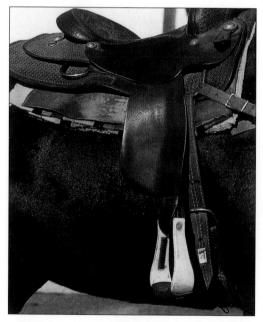

▌ ABOVE
The Australian stock saddle is built for comfort and durability. The rider may spend several hours driving cattle on the plains, and the even spread of his weight in the saddle will become a significant factor for both horse and rider.

▌ ABOVE
The high front of the Western reining saddle prevents the rider being thrown forward and out of the saddle when the horse performs the dramatic reining halt, which is a feature of this riding style.

■ ABOVE
Endurance saddle. This is designed specifically for
long-distance riding, with the comfort of both horse
and rider in mind.

■ ABOVE
The deep seat makes the
Western pleasure saddle
comfortable and secure
for long-distance riding.

■ RIGHT
The elaborate parade saddle
features intricately detailed
leatherwork, and makes a
splendid sight at carnivals
and rodeos.

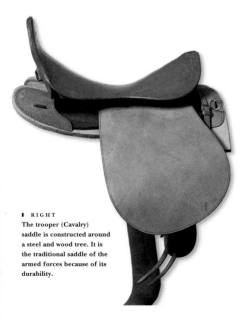

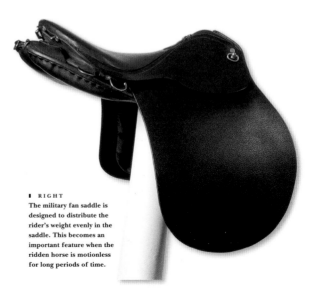

■ RIGHT
The trooper (Cavalry)
saddle is constructed around
a steel and wood tree. It is
the traditional saddle of the
armed forces because of its
durability.

■ RIGHT
The military fan saddle is
designed to distribute the
rider's weight evenly in the
saddle. This becomes an
important feature when the
ridden horse is motionless
for long periods of time.

Racing Saddles

Horse racing, and flat racing in particular, requires a highly unusual riding style that makes specific demands on the saddle.

The saddle used in flat racing is crouched over rather than sat on, and for this reason it has a flat seat and is fitted with very short stirrup leathers. **Leather racing saddles** are necessarily light; they come in a variety of weights, starting from as little as 325g/11oz. Saddles for National Hunt racing (racing over jumps) are heavier and larger in size than the saddles used for flat racing. **Synthetic racing saddles** are becoming increasingly popular for dirt and all-weather track racing, where the sand used for the track's surface can cause damage to leather tack.

As the name implies, **race exercise saddles** are used when exercising racehorses rather than when actually racing them. Because the question of weight does not apply, the exercise saddle is usually heavier and larger than the racing saddle, and comes with a full or half-tree in leather or synthetic material. The full-tree saddle illustrated features "todsloan" saddle flaps, named after the American jockey James Todhunter Sloan, who pioneered the style of riding with shorter stirrup leathers.

▮ LEFT
The flat seat and short stirrup leathers are characteristic of saddles used for flat racing. The jockey rides crouched over the saddle with his head tucked well in for a more streamlined position.

▮ RIGHT
Race exercise saddles are larger and heavier than racing saddles. Exercising the horse requires a more functional saddle than the lightweight type worn for the race.

Learner Saddles

For beginners taking their first lessons in equestrianism, a specially adapted saddle can be a huge advantage, not least because of the additional safety features which these saddles incorporate.

The **pony saddle**, designed for young children and smaller ponies, has removable panels to vary the amount by which the child is "wedged in", and a hand support for extra grip. The **felt-pad saddle** also includes the safety handle feature, and this can be very helpful for nervous children. The simple design consists of a soft felt pad with a leather covering and built-in **webbing girth and stirrup bars**.

The **Riding for the Disabled Association (RDA) saddle** will enable physically or mentally disabled children and adults to ride in safety. The loop fitted to the front of the saddle gives the rider something to hold on to without needing to grip and pull at the reins too tightly, thereby damaging the horse's mouth.

▮ LEFT
The pony saddle makes an ideal choice for small children who are just learning to ride.

▮ LEFT
The felt-pad saddle is a beginner's saddle for children. It consists of a soft felt pad with a leather covering and built-in webbing girth and stirrup bars.

▮ RIGHT
The design of the RDA saddle enables the physically and mentally disabled to ride with safety and confidence.

Ceremonial Saddles

The Royal Mews at Buckingham Palace in London houses a large collection of saddles, bridles and harnesses belonging to the Royal Family. Much of the saddlery and equipment in this beautiful collection is of a unique historical interest.

Queen Elizabeth II's love of horses is well known and many of the gifts she receives are related to the subject of riding. The Portuguese ceremonial bridle was presented with a saddle to HM the Queen by the Portuguese government on a state visit to Portugal in 1957. The bridle has solid silver bit and fittings.

The Alamo saddle was presented as a gift to the Queen from the actor John Wayne, who directed and starred in the film *The Alamo*. The saddle had been used by the actor during the making of the film. The design of the saddle is highly

ornate and features tooled fenders and decorated *tapaderos* (toe covers).

Although ladies traditionally sat to the near (left) side when riding side-saddle, it was not uncommon for young ladies learning to ride to use a saddle designed for riding on the off (right) side, as demonstrated by a pair of side-saddles belonging to Princess Mary.

Queen Victoria's side-saddle was used by the monarch in the latter half of the nineteenth century. To allow for a less restrictive riding style, the design features a pommel on either side of the saddle, so that the saddle can be ridden on either the near or the off side.

A hunting saddle used by the Prince Consort, HRH Prince Albert, during the mid-nineteenth century, is elaborately detailed in gold thread and features a

holster for carrying a pair of pistols, which in those days would have been carried for the prince's personal protection.

The Kaiser's bridle, a gift from Wilhelm II of Germany, has not been used since the diamond jubilee of Queen Victoria in 1898. The lavish design features gilt trim on the bits, solid gold buckles and gold thread embellishment on the bridoon rein.

The bridle worn by Queen Elizabeth II's horse, Burmese, at the annual military ceremony, Trooping the Colour, is based on the traditional military bridle and combines a headcollar with a bridle. The detailing on the bridle is gilt and the reins are decorated with gold thread. The elaborate saddlery traditionally worn for Trooping the Colour includes gilded stirrups on the Queen's side-saddle.

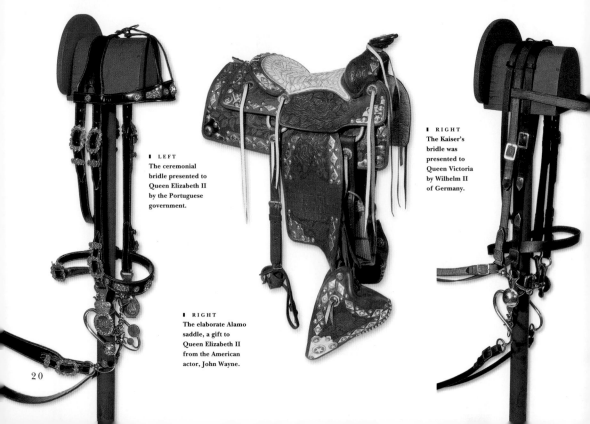

■ LEFT
The ceremonial bridle presented to Queen Elizabeth II by the Portuguese government.

■ RIGHT
The elaborate Alamo saddle, a gift to Queen Elizabeth II from the American actor, John Wayne.

■ RIGHT
The Kaiser's bridle was presented to Queen Victoria by Wilhelm II of Germany.

LEFT
A highly decorative
gilded stirrup from the
side-saddle ridden by
Queen Elizabeth II at
Trooping the Colour.

LEFT
A pair of side-saddles,
originally belonging
to Princess Mary, show
how the side-saddle
could be designed to
let the rider sit on the
off side.

BELOW
The military-style bridle worn
by Queen Elizabeth II's horse at
Trooping the Colour.

LEFT
A hunting saddle used
by the Prince Consort,
HRH Prince Albert, in
the nineteenth century.

BELOW
Traditional detailing on a bridle
worn by Queen Elizabeth II's horse
at ceremonial parades.

BELOW
Queen Victoria's side-
saddle, with the double
pommel design, allowed
the Queen to ride off
either side of the saddle.

Girths, Cinches and Surcingles

■ ABOVE
leather Atherstone girth

■ LEFT
Atherstone
girth with
elastic inserts

■ ABOVE
Balding girth

GIRTHS

Girths are used to keep the saddle in place on the horse's back. They are available in leather and synthetic materials: although expensive, leather girths are very durable if well cared for, while cotton and synthetic girths are cheaper and generally less hardwearing.

The **Atherstone girth** is padded and has a contoured shape to prevent it rubbing the horse's elbow. It is an ideal choice for general or competition use. The Atherstone is also available with strong elastic inserts at one or both ends, which allows the girth to stretch as the horse expands his ribcage when galloping. Take care not to overtighten an elasticated girth as it can still cause the horse discomfort, even though it stretches.

The **Balding girth** is made of a single piece of leather split into three. It was originally developed for polo ponies: the special shape helps to minimize chafing and girth galls.

The **three-fold leather girth** has become less common since the arrival of synthetic alternatives. It comprises a single piece of leather which is folded around a piece of oiled fabric. The girth is fitted with the open side away from the horse's elbow to prevent pinching. The oiled fabric helps to keep the leather supple.

The **Humane girth** has girth tabs which slide through special loops allowing the girth to move with the horse. The **Cottage Craft girth** is an inexpensive foam-padded, cotton girth which is both comfortable for the horse and easy to wash. **Cord girths**, made from thick cotton cords, have an open design which helps to reduce sweating while the cord strands themselves help to keep the girth in place.

Neoprene girths are available for general purpose and dressage saddles. The fabric (commonly used for wet suits) does not absorb sweat and helps to reduce rubbing. **Narrow-webbing girths** are often used on show horses and ponies, as they

are less obtrusive than traditional girths. They consist of two narrow strips of webbing and a small section of textured rubber to prevent the girth slipping.

The **dressage girth**, also known as the **Lonsdale girth**, is shorter than a traditional girth as it is designed for use with the dressage saddle, which has longer girth tabs (billets).

The **Fitzwilliam girth**, used with a side-saddle, features an extra balance strap to prevent the saddle from slipping. The **leather stud-guard girth** is useful when competing in show-jumping events or horse trials. It is designed to prevent horses fitted with studs from injuring themselves when they snatch up their forelegs over a fence.

Racing girths are made from elastic or from webbing with elastic inserts, allowing the horse the freedom to expand his ribcage at a full gallop.

Accessories can be fitted to the girth as aids to the horse's comfort. The **fleece girth sleeve (cover)**, a soft fleece or sheepskin sleeve which slides over the girth, helps to keep the girth clean and minimize rubbing and galling. **A girth extender** is a short leather strap used to lengthen the girth. **Girth (buckle) guards** are fitted over the **girth tabs (billets)** on the saddle to prevent the girth buckles from rubbing and damaging the saddle flap. **A stud guard** is a pad of leather which is fitted to a standard girth to protect the horse when jumping, in the same way as a

■ RIGHT three-fold leather girth
■ RIGHT Humane girth
■ RIGHT Cottage Craft girth
■ RIGHT neoprene girth
■ RIGHT Wintec girth
■ RIGHT dressage girth
■ RIGHT Cottage Craft dressage girth

▮ RIGHT
narrow-webbing show girth

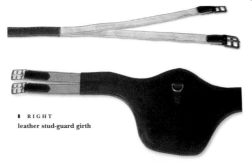

▮ RIGHT
leather stud-guard girth

▮ ABOVE
A racing saddle fitted with a surcingle.

▮ RIGHT
Western fleece cinch

▮ LEFT
A surcingle fitted
over the saddle
for cross-country
riding.

▮ RIGHT
Western strand (string) cinch

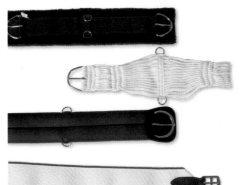

▮ RIGHT
neoprene cinch

▮ RIGHT
all-elastic racing girth

▮ RIGHT
racing girths

▮ RIGHT
Fitzwilliam side
saddle girth

stud-guard girth. The **sheepskin seat saver**
is fitted over the saddle to make it more
comfortable to ride for long periods of
time – ideal for endurance or trail-riding.

▮ LEFT
girth extender

CINCHES AND SURCINGLES
Western saddles are held in place with
cinches rather than girths. Cinches are
attached to the saddle by a large buckle
at each end and are available in a range
of materials: **neoprene** and **padded fleece
cinches** help to reduce chafing, while
strand cinches, made from cord or woven
horse hair, prevent the horse sweating.

Racing surcingles, in elastic or webbing
with an elastic insert, go over the top of
the saddle. They are used in addition to
a racing girth to provide extra security
in the event of the racing girth breaking.
For the same reason, the **overgirth** or
surcingle is fitted over the saddle for the
cross-country phase of horse trials.

▮ LEFT
all-elastic racing surcingle

▮ LEFT
tubular racing surcingle

▮ ABOVE
fleece girth sleeve
(cover)

▮ LEFT
leather stud guard

▮ RIGHT
sheepskin seat
saver

▮ RIGHT
girth (buckle) guard

Breastplates and Cruppers

BREASTPLATES AND BREASTGIRTHS

The breastplate and breastgirth are designed to stop the saddle slipping back, and are especially useful for high impact disciplines such as galloping or jumping.

The sturdy **hunting breastplate** is made from leather or leather and elastic. Two straps are attached to the D rings on the saddle, while a strap passes through the horse's front legs and loops around the girth. A ring at the chest allows a running martingale to be fitted if necessary. The **racing breastplate** is a lightweight version of the hunting type, while the **Western breastplate**, made of tooled leather, is heavier than the English type and is used with the Western saddle only.

The breastgirth is a simple strap which is passed around the horse's chest and attached to the girth on either side of the saddle. The **leather breastgirth** is commonly used on polo ponies, while the **elasticated** or **Aintree breastgirth** allows for the movement of the horse during strenuous exercise, in particular when jumping across country. The **continental breastgirth** is similar to a normal breastgirth but is fitted to the saddle D rings rather than to the girth.

A **sheepskin sleeve (cover)** can be fitted over the chest strap of a breastgirth to prevent it from rubbing the horse.

The **neck strap** is a useful attachment for novice riders or for those training young horses. A strong leather strap, such as a stirrup leather, is fitted around the base of the horse's neck. It is useful for jumping as it gives the rider something to hold on to without pulling at the reins and risking damage to the horse's mouth.

CRUPPERS

A crupper can be fitted to prevent the saddle from slipping forward and is generally only needed on ponies. A strap is passed under the tail and attached to the back of the saddle.

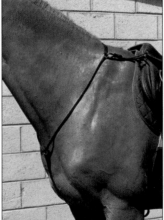

■ ABOVE
The hunting breastplate is used to prevent the saddle slipping back when the horse is galloping and jumping.

■ LEFT
The racing breastplate is a lightweight alternative to the hunting type, but it is designed to serve the same purpose.

■ BELOW
Western breastplate

Polo ponies are often fitted with leather breastgirths.

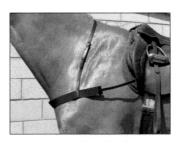

The modern elasticated breastgirth allows the horse greater freedom of movement.

The continental breastgirth is attached to the D rings of the saddle, rather than to the girth.

A sheepskin sleeve (cover) can be fitted over a breastgirth to prevent the strap rubbing the horse.

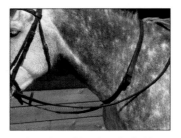

A neck strap is a useful attachment for the rider to hold on to when jumping or galloping, and can help make a nervous rider feel more secure.

HOW TO ATTACH A BREASTGIRTH

Attach the strap from the breastgirth to the girth just under the buckle, above the numnah strap to prevent it slipping down. Pass it under the first strap and round the second strap.

▐ ABOVE
A crupper is often worn by ponies and smaller horses to prevent the saddle slipping forwards.

FITTING A LEATHER BREASTPLATE

1 When the breastplate is in place, check that the fit allows room for a palm's width at the chest.

2 You should be able to fit four fingers under the strap which passes over the neck.

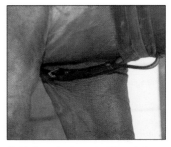

3 The breastplate keeper should be pushed tightly up to the girth so that there is no loop in which the horse could catch his foot.

Stirrups

Stirrups, also known as irons, are available in a variety of styles but are almost always made from stainless steel, which is extremely strong. For safety, the stirrup should be wide enough to allow about 1–1.5cm/$\frac{1}{2}$in on either side of the rider's foot to avoid the foot getting caught in the stirrup in the event of a fall.

The most common English stirrup is the **Prussian side open bottom**, also known as a **hunting iron**. Very useful for dressage and jumping are heavier models such as the **fillis stirrup**, which give the rider more balance. The **off-set fillis** is a popular choice for jumping. The eye of the stirrup is set to the inside, which encourages the knee and thigh to be pressed into the saddle for extra grip.

Alternatives to steel become necessary when weight is important. Contemporary choices include the **carbon-fibre stirrup** which is both light and strong, and features graphite treads for extra grip. **Polymer** and **Flexi-ride stirrups** are designed specifically for endurance and trail-riding. The rubberized material absorbs concussion, enhancing the rider's comfort when riding for long periods of time. **Cradle-bottom racing stirrups**, which are designed purely for racing, are made from lightweight aluminium.

Western stirrups consist of a wooden or Ralide frame covered in leather; a more decorative design is made from inlaid wood. For parades, a toe cover called a *tapadero* can be fitted to the stirrup. The **side-saddle stirrup** features a round eye through which the stirrup leather passes, allowing greater flexibility of movement for the rider's leg.

Rubber treads can be fitted into stirrups to provide extra grip for muddy boots or when riding in wet weather. The treads lie flat inside the stirrup, although angled or wedged treads are also available for dressage and jumping.

■ ABOVE
Prussian side open bottom stirrups are the traditional English riding stirrups.

■ ABOVE
Fillis stirrups are solid and heavy, and are used to help the rider balance in the saddle.

■ ABOVE
The eye of the off-set fillis stirrup is set to the inside, pressing the knee towards the saddle.

■ ABOVE
Cradle-bottom racing stirrups are made from lightweight aluminium.

■ ABOVE
leather-covered Western stirrup

■ ABOVE
inlaid wood Western stirrups

■ ABOVE
Toe covers can be fitted to ordinary
stirrups. They are commonly used in
endurance and trail-riding events and
will prevent the rider's foot sliding
through and getting stuck in the
stirrup.

■ ABOVE
Polymer and Flexi-ride stirrups are
designed to increase foot comfort
when endurance or trail-riding.

■ LEFT
Carbon-fibre
stirrups are
lightweight but
extremely strong.

■ ABOVE
The round eye of the side-saddle
stirrup allows the lower leg greater
flexibility.

■ RIGHT
Rubber treads are fitted to
stirrups to provide extra grip.

SAFETY STIRRUPS

In the event of a fall, the rider risks serious injury if his foot becomes caught in the stirrup. Safety stirrups are designed to prevent this by allowing the foot to be quickly released from the stirrup.

The **Australian Simplex** or **bent-leg stirrup** has a bent outer leg on the iron, encouraging the early release of the foot. The **Peacock safety stirrup** has a strong band of rubber fitted to the outside of the stirrup, which is pulled off if the foot gets caught. The **precision riding stirrup** is a new design which self-aligns to the position of your foot to increase comfort and security.

STIRRUP LEATHERS

English leathers are traditionally made from top-quality English dressed hides. **Extending leathers** have a small hook attachment which allows the stirrup to be lengthened for mounting. **Racing leathers** are lightweight and made from leather and nylon web. **Jumping** or **double-sided stirrup leathers** are reinforced with nylon to strengthen the leather and prevent it from stretching. The **side-saddle leather** has a hook adjustment to alter the length at the base, near the stirrup. **Dressage leathers** are a smart single thickness of leather with a buckle at the base, allowing the legs to be carried closer to the horse.

Australian Simplex safety or bent-leg stirrups. The bent leg of the iron is fitted to the outside.

Peacock safety stirrups. In the event of a fall, the rubber is pulled off to release the foot.

Precision riding stirrups self-align for safety and comfort.

Jumping stirrup leathers, also known as double-sided stirrup leathers, are reinforced with nylon for extra strength under extreme pressure.

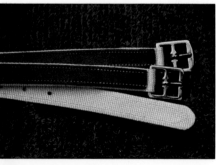

Top to bottom: synthetic stirrup leathers, racing stirrup leathers, English stirrup leathers

Side-saddle stirrup leathers.

Numnahs and Saddle Cloths

Numnahs and saddle cloths are fitted under the saddle to stop the saddle rubbing the horse's back and to absorb the concussion caused by movement. They help to keep the underside of the saddle clean by absorbing sweat and grease from the horse's body. Numnahs are saddle-shaped whereas a saddle pad or cloth is normally square or rectangular. A numnah or saddle cloth should never be used to make an ill-fitting saddle fit, and if not kept scrupulously clean they can rub the horse's back, leading to sores and even skin diseases.

Lightweight **quilted cotton numnahs** are ideal for protecting the saddle from sweat. They are held in place with straps which go round the girth and girth tabs. Available to fit general purpose and dressage saddles, they come in a variety of colours, although white is traditional for competitions.

The materials from which numnahs and saddle pads are made are chosen for their comfort-inducing properties. The **wither pad** is a small, oval pad in fleece or sheepskin which is placed between the wither and the saddle. The **pure new wool numnah**, fully washable with a cotton backing, is designed to relieve and prevent pressure sores. The **sheepskin numnah** absorbs impact and allows heat from the horse's body to pass through it. The **non-slip numnah**, made from neoprene, is designed to absorb concussion and to prevent the saddle from slipping.

Modern choices often include unique features which make them more attractive to the rider. The **Poly pad** is a thick, quilted pad which provides extra protection for the horse's back. Unlike many other numnahs or saddle cloths, it stays in place without the need for straps or loops. The **Coolback numnah** or saddle cloth features a special lining which draws sweat away from the horse's back. The **Proteq saddle pad** is a unique concept,

LEFT
A saddle cloth or numnah for a general purpose saddle.

BELOW
A Poly pad is a thick quilted pad which provides extra protection from the saddle. It is also available as a wither pad.

ABOVE
A quilted cotton saddle cloth and numnah for a dressage saddle.

LEFT
Navajo fleece pad

BELOW
pure wool numnah (*left*) and sheepskin numnah

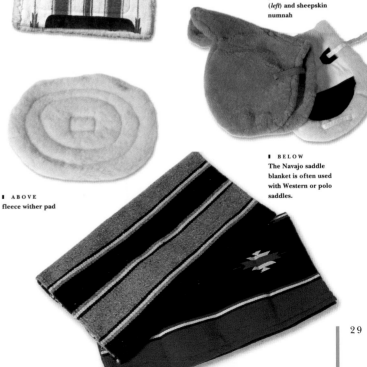

ABOVE
fleece wither pad

BELOW
The Navajo saddle blanket is often used with Western or polo saddles.

incorporating thousands of tiny poly-styrene beads. When the saddle is in place the air is pumped out of the pad, so that the beads mould to the configuration between the saddle and the horse's back.

Western and polo saddles are traditionally fitted with the **Navajo saddle blanket**. The **Navajo fleece pad** is a Western blanket pad with a fleece lining.

The **racing weight cloth** is fitted between the numnah and the saddle. It features a series of pockets in which lead weights can be placed to ensure that the rider is carrying the correct weight for the race. Weight cloths are also used in the speed and endurance phases of horse trials.

New products designed to fit between the saddle and the numnah now make use of highly effective synthetic materials. These include the **Pro-lite relief pad**, which incorporates a visco-elastic gel and latex rubber to absorb impact, and the **gel pad**, which contains thermoplastic elastomer gel for shock absorbency. Flat or moulded **shock-absorbing pads** can be placed under the saddle to help distribute the rider's weight more evenly over the horse's back.

▌ ABOVE
Aerborn Coolback numnah. This saddle cloth has a special lining which absorbs sweat from the horse's back.

▌ ABOVE
The gel pad contains a thermoplastic elastomer gel to aid shock absorbency.

▌ ABOVE
Placed under the saddle, the moulded shock-absorbing pad helps to distribute the rider's weight evenly.

▌ ABOVE
The flat shock-absorbing pad is used to help distribute the rider's weight along the horse's back.

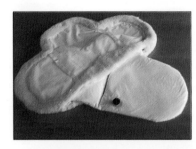

▌ LEFT
The Proteq saddle pad incorporates thousands of tiny polystyrene beads, which help mould the pad to the horse's back.

▌ ABOVE
The Pro-lite relief pad uses visco-elastic gel and latex rubber to absorb impact and concussion.

▌ ABOVE
Lead weights can be added to the pockets of the weight cloth to ensure the jockey carries the correct weight for the race.

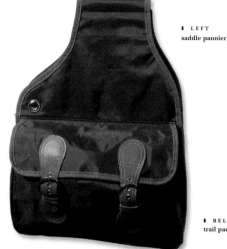

Saddle Bags

Saddle bags, pouches or panniers are lightweight bags which can be fitted to the saddle, positioned behind it and hung over either side of the horse. They are functional accessories used to carry the provisions needed on rides of several hours or more.

The **trail pad**, a fleece pad incorporated into a canvas cloth with pockets, is ideal for endurance and long-distance pleasure rides. The fleece numnah sits comfortably on the horse, while the canvas overlay is suitably sturdy.

As its name suggests, the **hunting canteen** was traditionally used to carry the refreshments necessary for a day's fox hunting. The smart leather pouch is just the right size to hold a flask of warming liquor.

Argentinian saddle bags are handwoven from wool in traditional patterns. They are used by *gauchos* to carry food when riding for days at a time out on the *pampas*.

▮ BELOW
trail pad

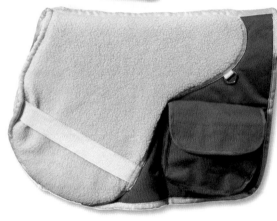

▮ LEFT
hunting canteen

▮ ABOVE
Argentinian saddle bag

Saddle Care

A good saddle is a costly piece of equipment and it is important to look after it properly, not only because it is expensive to repair but because a damaged saddle may harm your horse's back.

HOW TO CARRY A SADDLE

◼ LEFT
The saddle should be carried in either of the two ways shown: over the forearm with the back of the saddle nearest the elbow (*far left*), or against the side of the body with the hand holding on to the pommel (*left*).

HOW TO STORE A SADDLE

Once you have removed the saddle from the horse, it can be placed over a fence or saddle rack before being returned to the tack room. (If you leave the saddle over a stable door, the horse will most probably nudge it off.)

You can also put the saddle on the ground, pommel down and with the seat facing the wall. Place the girth between the pommel and the ground to protect the leather.

Saddles are best kept on saddle racks in a clean and dry tack room – damp conditions will damage the leather. Do not leave sweaty numnahs or girths attached to the saddle; remove and clean them before putting them away separately.

HOW TO CLEAN A SADDLE

1 Place the saddle on a stand. Remove the stirrup leathers, girth and numnah. With warm water and a dampened sponge, work all over the saddle removing any mud, sweat and general dirt. Take care not to let the leather get too wet.

2 Whilst cleaning, check the saddle for wear and tear. Pay particular attention to the stitching, especially where the girth tabs (billets) are joined to the saddle.

3 Don't forget to clean the underside of the saddle as this can get sweaty even if a numnah or saddle cloth has been used.

4 Allow the leather to dry slightly before applying the saddle soap. Use a fresh sponge and work the saddle soap into the leather with a circular rubbing motion. Cover the entire surface of the saddle, including under the saddle flaps.

SADDLING UP

1 Place a numnah or saddle cloth on the horse's back, making sure it is positioned sufficiently high up the horse's withers.

2 Lift the saddle over the horse's back and carefully lower it into position on top of the numnah or saddle cloth. Ensure both saddle flaps are lying flat against the horse's sides.

3 Pull the numnah or saddle cloth up into the gullet of the saddle so that it is clear of the horse's withers.

4 Numnahs usually have straps to anchor them to the saddle and stop them from slipping. Attach the top straps to the saddle's girth tabs (billets) through which the girth is fitted above the girth guard before doing up the girth.

5 Buckle the girth to the off side (right) of the saddle first and pass it through the bottom strap on the numnah. Move back to the near side (left) of the horse, reach underneath him and take hold of the girth.

6 Pass the girth through the retaining strap on the numnah before buckling to the saddle girth tabs on the near side.

5 Remove dirt and grease from the stirrup leathers with a sponge. Apply the saddle soap and check the stitching for wear. Check that the leathers have not stretched: because we mount from the near side, one leather will become longer than the other if they are not switched regularly.

7 Tighten up the girth gradually (it should be equal on both sides) until there is just room to fit the flat of your hand between the girth and the horse's side. Picking up the horse's feet, one at a time, and pulling them forward will also help you to judge if the girth is comfortable for the horse.

8 Once the girth has been tightened, slide the buckle guard down over the girth buckles to prevent them from rubbing against and damaging the saddle flaps. Slide your hand round the horse's belly under the girth to ensure that there are no wrinkles in the horse's skin.

Bridles and Bits

Along with the saddle, the bridle and bit are the most important pieces of equipment for the ridden horse. Combined with the rider's legs, voice and body position, the bridle and bit provide that important line of communication which allows you to control the horse.

Bridles are traditionally made of leather. However, synthetic bridles, which come in a choice of vivid colours, are becoming much more popular, especially in the sports of flat racing and endurance riding.

The variety of bits available can be bewildering, and choosing the right bit for a horse is almost a science in itself. To simplify matters, bits are divided into five groups which are categorized by their action, based on the area of the horse's head to which pressure is applied. The five groups are: snaffles, doubles, pelhams, gag snaffles and bitless bridles. It is important to make an accurate judgment over your choice of bit: a bit that is too weak will result in the rider having no control over the horse, while one that is too severe will encourage the horse to fight against it.

▮ OPPOSITE
A correctly "put up" bridle, with the throat latch fastened in a figure-of-eight.

▮ LEFT
A Rugby pelham fitted with a curb chain.

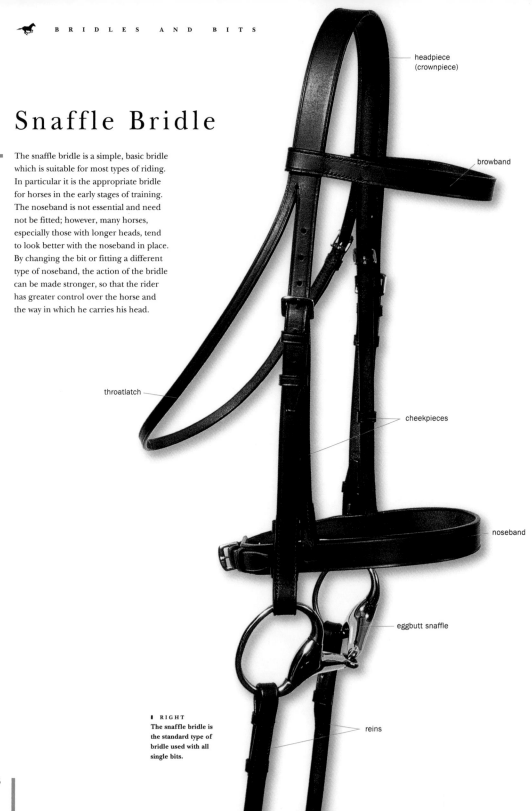

headpiece
(crownpiece)

browband

Snaffle Bridle

The snaffle bridle is a simple, basic bridle
which is suitable for most types of riding.
In particular it is the appropriate bridle
for horses in the early stages of training.
The noseband is not essential and need
not be fitted; however, many horses,
especially those with longer heads, tend
to look better with the noseband in place.
By changing the bit or fitting a different
type of noseband, the action of the bridle
can be made stronger, so that the rider
has greater control over the horse and
the way in which he carries his head.

throatlatch

cheekpieces

noseband

eggbutt snaffle

▌ RIGHT
The snaffle bridle is
the standard type of
bridle used with all
single bits.

reins

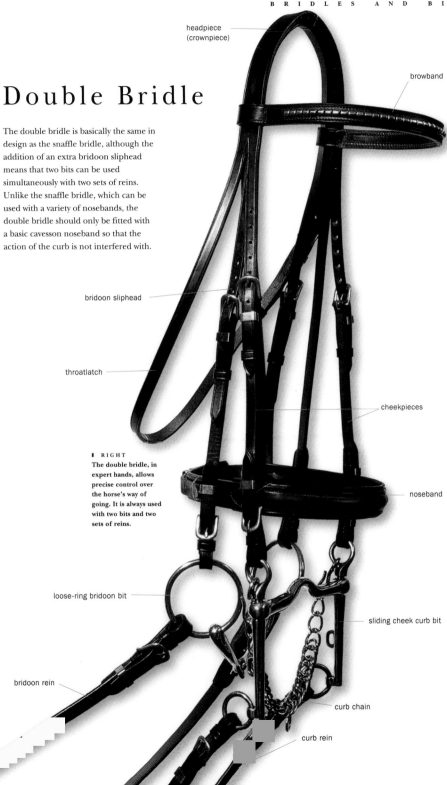

headpiece
(crownpiece)

browband

Double Bridle

The double bridle is basically the same in
design as the snaffle bridle, although the
addition of an extra bridoon sliphead
means that two bits can be used
simultaneously with two sets of reins.
Unlike the snaffle bridle, which can be
used with a variety of nosebands, the
double bridle should only be fitted with
a basic cavesson noseband so that the
action of the curb is not interfered with.

bridoon sliphead

throatlatch

cheekpieces

■ RIGHT
**The double bridle, in
expert hands, allows
precise control over
the horse's way of
going. It is always used
with two bits and two
sets of reins.**

noseband

loose-ring bridoon bit

sliding cheek curb bit

bridoon rein

curb chain

curb rein

Western Bridle

The traditional Western bridle is fastened with narrow leather thongs, which enabled the cowboy to carry out running repairs on any items of broken tack himself when he was miles from the nearest saddler. Western bridles are referred to as either "one-ear" or "split-ear". The headpiece (crownpiece) of a split-ear bridle is made from a single piece of leather which has slits cut into it to fit over each ear. This is to prevent the bridle from being pulled off accidentally. The one-ear bridle incorporates a definite loop which fits over one of the horse's ears. The reins of the Western bridle are not joined at the end. This is to avoid the risk of the horse getting a foot caught in the reins if they trail on the ground.

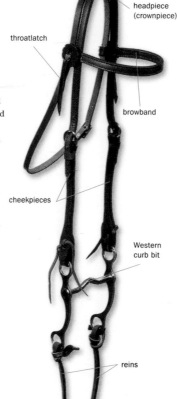

headpiece
(crownpiece)

throatlatch

browband

cheekpieces

Western
curb bit

reins

▮ **RIGHT**
split-ear Western bridle

▮ **BELOW**
one-ear Western bridle

Endurance 2-in-1 Bridle

The endurance bridle is a combination of a headcollar (crownpiece) and a standard bridle. The cheekpieces and reins can be quickly unclipped to leave just the headcollar in place. The headcollar can also be ridden as a Scawbrig, a type of bitless bridle, by attaching the reins to the noseband. The endurance bridle (also known as the combination bridle) has proved popular with endurance riders because of its practical design: the bit can be removed quickly to give the horse a drink during competition, while the reins very usefully double as a lead rope.

▮ **RIGHT**
endurance 2-in-1 bridle

THE MAIN POINTS OF CONTROL

Bits, bitless bridles and certain types of nosebands will all act on specific parts of the horse's head.

The poll – the headpiece (crownpiece) of the bridle applies pressure here when a gag or curb bit is used.

The nose – bitless bridles and specific types of nosebands affect the nose.

The mouthcorners – snaffle bits bring pressure on the corners of the horse's mouth and lips.

Side of the face – bits with full cheeks, D rings or large racing rings affect this area.

Curb groove – the curb chain fitted with a pelham or Weymouth bit affects the curb groove.

Roof of the mouth – bits with ported mouthpieces affect this area.

Tongue – all bits apply pressure to the tongue.

Bars – all bits affect the bars, a sensitive part of the horse's mouth between the incisors and premolar teeth.

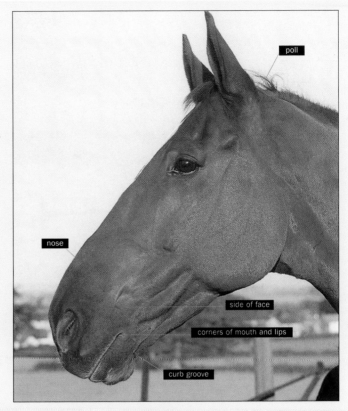

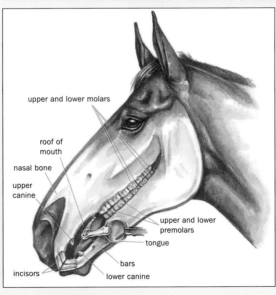

Snaffle Bits

The snaffle bit is the largest of the five bit groups. It contains a wide variety of different types of bit which vary in strength of action from very mild to severe. Snaffle bits act on the tongue, the bars and the corners of the mouth; some also act on the roof of the mouth. Snaffle bits encourage the horse to raise his head and bring it back towards your hands for greater control. In its basic form the snaffle is the most commonly used bit for horses in the early stages of schooling. Any well-schooled horse should go happily in a snaffle bit.

While all snaffles have the same basic action, different cheek- and mouthpieces will affect the action and severity of the bit. The single-jointed **eggbutt snaffle** has rounded edges where the rings join the mouthpiece to prevent the lips being pinched. The fixed cheek rings keep the bit relatively still in the horse's mouth.

The rings of the **loose-ring snaffle** allow the bit to move more freely in the horse's mouth, which some horses prefer. This type should be fitted slightly wider than the eggbutt snaffle, and can have rubber bit guards fitted over the rings to prevent it from pinching the horse's lips.

The **full-cheek snaffle** has extended cheekpieces which prevent the bit from sliding through the horse's mouth, and help to steer the horse by bringing pressure against the side of his face. This type of bit should be fitted with leather **fulmer keepers** attached to the cheekpieces of the bridle, to hold the bit still in the mouth and to prevent a cheekpiece from accidentally getting stuck up the horse's nostril. The **fulmer snaffle** is similar to the full-cheek but has loose, rather than fixed, bit rings.

The **half-spoon cheek snaffle** has spoon-shaped cheeks which extend downwards to put pressure on the outside of the lower jaw, helping with steering. The **D-ring snaffle** is often used on racehorses in preference to a fulmer

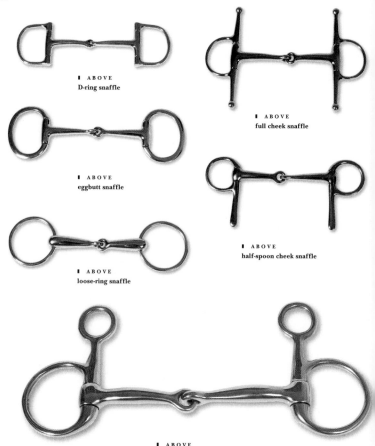

■ ABOVE
D-ring snaffle

■ ABOVE
full cheek snaffle

■ ABOVE
eggbutt snaffle

■ ABOVE
half-spoon cheek snaffle

■ ABOVE
loose-ring snaffle

■ ABOVE
Filet Baucher snaffle

snaffle. Like the fulmer, the shape of the cheekpieces prevents the bit being pulled through the mouth. By bringing pressure on the sides of the horse's face it can also help to steer the horse.

The **Filet Baucher** or **hanging cheek snaffle** has separate rings to which the cheekpieces of the bridle are attached so that the bit is suspended in the horse's mouth. Unlike other snaffles, the cheekpieces will exert some pressure on the horse's poll.

■ ABOVE
fulmer keepers

TYPES OF MOUTHPIECE

Snaffle bits come with a variety of mouthpieces which vary in the severity of their action.

The **straight bar mouthpiece** usually comes with non-riding bits such as stallion-showing bits or in-hand bits, and acts primarily on the tongue and lips.

The **mullen mouth** is a mild, simple unjointed mouthpiece, more curved than the straight bar. The mullen mouth rests on the bars of the mouth, exerting less pressure on the corners of the mouth and a more uniform pressure on the tongue.

When pressure is applied to the reins, the **single-jointed bit** squeezes the corners of the mouth in a nutcracker action, as well as applying pressure to the bars, the tongue and the roof of the mouth. Single-jointed snaffles have either a narrow, solid mouthpiece or fatter hollow mouthpiece (this latter type is known as the German snaffle). As a general rule of thumb, the fatter the mouthpiece, the milder its action.

Double-jointed mouthpieces feature a central link, which comes in different shapes and sizes. The nutcracker action is less severe than with single-jointed bits. However, these bits still act on the bars and corners of the horse's mouth.

The **French link** has a kidney-shaped link in the middle of the mouthpiece. It increases the flexibility of the bit, stops the horse from leaning and encourages him to soften his mouth.

The **Dr Bristol** incorporates a flat plate link which is much more severe in action than the French link. It is used in vigorous competition events such as jumping or cross-country. The plate applies strong pressure on the horse's tongue unless the head is carried in the position needed for the rider to control him. No small amount of pain will be inflicted on the horse if the bit is misused and it should only be used by experienced riders on particularly boisterous horses.

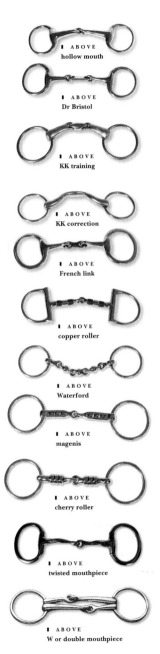

▮ A B O V E
hollow mouth

▮ A B O V E
Dr Bristol

▮ A B O V E
KK training

▮ A B O V E
KK correction

▮ A B O V E
French link

▮ A B O V E
copper roller

▮ A B O V E
Waterford

▮ A B O V E
magenis

▮ A B O V E
cherry roller

▮ A B O V E
twisted mouthpiece

▮ A B O V E
W or double mouthpiece

The **KK training bit** has a central lozenge-shaped link which is designed to shift pressure away from the lips and corners towards the centre of the horse's mouth to give a milder bit action.

The **Waterford bit** has a multi-jointed mouthpiece made up of a series of bulbous links. Because of the number of links, this mouthpiece is extremely flexible, which discourages the horse from leaning on it.

Roller mouthpieces feature a series of rollers in either steel or steel and copper. Because of the movement, these mouthpieces are used to discourage the horse from leaning on the rider's hands. There are two main types of roller mouthpieces: the **magenis** is a strong bit which features small rollers set into a squared-off mouthpiece; the **cherry roller** has rollers across the length of the mouthpiece and will encourage the horse to play with the bit, keeping his mouth relaxed. The more rounded shape of the mouthpiece means it has a kinder action than the magenis. Another roller mouthpiece, the **copper roller**, is similar to the cherry roller except that the rollers alternate between copper and steel. The copper is included to encourage the horse to salivate and relax his jaw.

The **twisted mouthpiece** is very severe, putting sharp pressure on the horse's tongue and the corners of his mouth.

Ported mouthpieces allow more room for the horse's tongue than other types of mouthpiece, while placing more contact on the bars. Bits with a high port will also act on the roof of the horse's mouth, causing the horse to raise his head.

The **KK correction bit** is a training bit made from Aurigan (a copper alloy) and is designed for strong, pulling horses.

The **W** or **double mouthpiece** has two thin, single-jointed mouthpieces attached to a set of bit rings. Strong bits like this are best left to expert riders because of the damage they can do to the horse's mouth.

Double Bits

Double bits are a combination of two bits:
the **bridoon** (a snaffle bit) and a **curb bit**,
also known as a **Weymouth**, which is fitted
with a curb chain. The bridoon acts in
exactly the same way as the snaffle, raising
the horse's head, while the curb bit acts
on the horse's poll and curb groove.
Combining these two bits in one bridle
enables you to fine tune your horse's head
and neck carriage. A double bridle
is used on horses who are already well
schooled, particularly for dressage. It is
also considered the correct bridle for
the show ring. The curb bit comes with
a mullen or ported mouthpiece. The
length of the cheekpieces on curb bits
varies but in general, the longer the
cheekpieces, the greater the poll pressure.

■ **ABOVE**
An eggbutt bridoon
(top) **with a fixed-**
cheek Weymouth
(below).

■ **LEFT**
A loose-ring bridoon
(top) **with a sliding-**
cheek Weymouth curb
(below).

Pelham Bits

The pelham is a compromise between a snaffle and a double bridle, combining the actions of both. As well as exerting pressure on the horse's mouth, pelhams also act on the poll and curb groove. Unlike the double bridle, it has only one mouthpiece and can be ridden with pelham roundings, the short pieces of leather linking the top and bottom rings, so that only one set of reins is needed (although it is more correct to ride with two). It is ideal for a show horse whose mouth is too small for a double bridle.

The **mullen-mouthed pelham** is the most popular pelham mouthpiece and

also the mildest in action. The **jointed pelham** is very strong, the jointed mouthpiece having a direct action on the horse's tongue. The **Rugby pelham** has a loose-ring link for the bridoon rein, and as a consequence it brings greater pressure on the horse's curb and poll. The **Scamperdale pelham** is ideal for horses with fleshy lips. The mouthpiece is shaped so that it bends back at either end. This helps to keep the cheekpieces of the bit away from the horse's lips to prevent chafing. Unlike most other pelhams, the **globe pelham** is fitted with only one set of reins, which are attached to the lower rings.

The **kimblewick**, also known as the **Kimberwicke** or **Spanish jumping bit**, comes into the category of pelhams although it has less leverage action than a pelham and is ridden with only one set of reins. The **slotted-cheek kimblewick** (shown here with a hinged, copper, quarter-moon mouthpiece) enables you to choose at what height to attach the reins. The lower they are fitted, the greater the curb action of the bit. The **rounded-cheek kimblewick** has a similar action to a snaffle bit when the rider's hands are held high: lowering the hands emphasizes the curb action.

■ ABOVE
jointed pelham

■ ABOVE
Scamperdale pelham

■ ABOVE
Uxeter hinged copper kimblewick

■ ABOVE
mullen-mouthed pelham

■ RIGHT
globe pelham

■ ABOVE
Cambridge mouth kimblewick

■ ABOVE
Rugby pelham

■ ABOVE
pelham roundings

■ ABOVE
slotted-cheek kimblewick

Gag Snaffles

This group of bits encourages the horse to raise his head by raising the bit in his mouth, as well as acting on the corners of the mouth and the poll. Gag snaffles are popular bits for strong, fit horses ridden across country and for those who like to put their heads down and gallop off. Like the pelham, the gag snaffle should be fitted with two sets of reins (although they can be used with only one set, attached to the roundings). One set is attached to the bit ring like a snaffle, the second set to the roundings which pass from the cheekpieces through the bit rings. This enables the rider to utilize the strong gag action only when it is actually needed.

The **Balding gag** has loose-ring cheekpieces through which gag roundings pass. The **Cheltenham gag** is similar in design but features eggbutt bit rings. With both types of gag, the larger the bit ring, the more severe the bit's action.

The **half-ring**, or **Duncan gag**, is a particularly strong type of gag as it can only be used with one set of reins, which is fitted to the gag roundings.

The **Dutch gag**, also called the **continental** or **three-ring gag**, can be used with one or two sets of reins. The bridle cheekpieces are attached to the top rings to produce poll pressure. The reins can be fitted to any of the three lower rings: the lower the reins are fitted, the stronger the leverage action on the horse's mouth.

The **American gag** should also be used with two sets of reins (one set fitted to the central rings and the other fitted to the lower rings). As the gag (lower) rein is used, the mouthpiece slides up the cheekpieces, encouraging the horse to raise his head.

Gag roundings, or **running cheeks**, are leather or nylon straps which are attached to the cheekpieces of the bridle and then passed through the bit rings and attached directly to the reins. As the rider takes a contact on the reins, the bit slides up the roundings and the horse's head is raised.

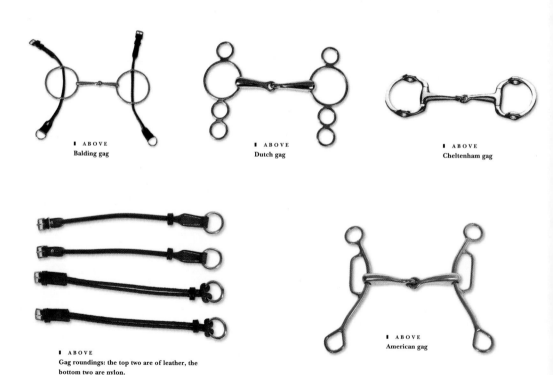

▮ ABOVE
Balding gag

▮ ABOVE
Dutch gag

▮ ABOVE
Cheltenham gag

▮ ABOVE
Gag roundings: the top two are of leather, the bottom two are nylon.

▮ ABOVE
American gag

The Bitless Bridle

Although not a bit at all, bitless bridles, also known as hackamores, make up the fifth bit group. Instead of acting on the horse's mouth, bitless bridles apply pressure to the horse's nose as well as to the poll and curb groove. They can be used on horses who have injured their mouths but need to be kept in ridden work. Although bitless bridles have no influence on the horse's mouth, they can still be severe in inexperienced hands.

The **English pattern** or **Blair hackamore** has a padded noseband, metal cheeks and a leather curb strap (which is fitted slightly higher than a normal curb chain). Take care when fitting the English hackamore: if it is too high, the cheekpieces may rub the horse's cheeks; if it is too low, it can interfere with his breathing.

The **German hackamore** has a rubber-covered metal noseband, often worn padded with sheepskin, and a curb chain. The longer cheekpieces of the German hackamore have a stronger leverage action than the English pattern. Both types of hackamore can be used in conjunction with a bit by simply adding an extra sliphead to the bridle.

The **bosal** forms an integral part of Western training and riding. It is usually made from plaited (braided) rawhide and is used with a normal or one-ear bridle. The reins are attached directly to the "heel" knot at the back of the bridle.

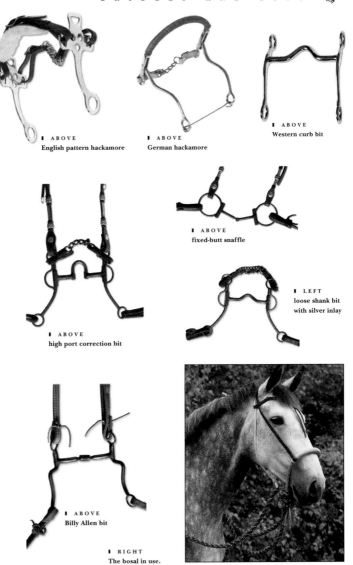

I ABOVE
English pattern hackamore

I ABOVE
German hackamore

I ABOVE
Western curb bit

I ABOVE
fixed-butt snaffle

I LEFT
loose shank bit with silver inlay

I ABOVE
high port correction bit

I ABOVE
Billy Allen bit

I RIGHT
The bosal in use.

WESTERN BITS

With their long cheekpieces and ported mouthpieces **Western curb bits** can appear severe, but in practice the Western horse is ridden with such a light contact that this is not the case. The horse is systematically trained, first using a bosal, then a combination of bosal and bit, and finally a bit alone. Western riders traditionally ride with just the weight of the rein itself maintaining the contact. Western bits are usually made out of sweet iron. This is

"warmer" than stainless steel, and the rusting that naturally occurs encourages the horse to salivate.

The **high port correction bit** has loose shanks which allow the cheekpieces to swivel at the butt of the mouthpiece. The high port acts on the roof of the horse's mouth when a contact is taken.

The **low port bit** has silver inlay, a chain and a plaited (braided) nylon curb strap. The angle of the shank on the bit determines the severity of the leverage

action, with a more angled shank giving a milder leverage action.

The **Billy Allen bit** has a jointed mouthpiece with a central roller, which lessens the nutcracker action of the mouthpiece. It is used as a transitional bit between the shank snaffle and a curb bit.

The **fixed-butt snaffle** is similar in action to an English eggbutt snaffle – the fixed butt keeps the bit still in the horse's mouth while the single joint has a nutcracker action on the horse's tongue.

45

Unusual Bits

There will always be bits that do not fit neatly into specific categories or those which have evolved with a specific sport in mind. Here are a few examples.

The **citation bit** forms part of a combination bit and bridling system called a Norton bridle. It has two mouthpieces, the thinner of which is attached directly to the noseband via the links on the bit rings. This is a highly specialized bit and bridle and is strictly for experienced hands only.

The **scourier** or **Cornish bit** has two sets of bit rings, one of which passes through holes in the mouthpiece. The inside rings are attached to the bridle while the outer

rings are attached to the reins. This, combined with a grooved mouthpiece, results in a very severe bit.

The **Wilson snaffle**, like the scourier, has two pairs of bit rings. This bit is used for driving. Its action is similar to that of the scourier – pressure applied to the reins causes the bit rings to squeeze on the sides of the horse's mouth.

The **wind-sucking bridoon** or **flute bit** has a wide, hollow mouthpiece pierced with a series of small holes. It is designed to stop the horse from gulping down air when crib biting or wind-sucking.

The **tongue bit** incorporates a flat metal plate which prevents the horse from evading the bit by getting his tongue over the mouthpiece.

The **butterfly bit** is not a bit as such, but an attachment which clips on to the mouthpiece of an existing bit to increase the severity of its action.

The **loose-ring racing snaffle** has much larger bit rings than normal snaffles. The larger rings prevent the bit from being pulled through the horse's mouth. They can also help to steer the horse in a chosen direction by bringing pressure on the side of the face.

❚ ABOVE
scourier

❚ ABOVE
citation

❚ ABOVE
mouthing or breaking bit

❚ ABOVE
Wilson snaffle

❚ ABOVE
tongue bit

❚ ABOVE
wind-sucking bridoon

❚ ABOVE
loose-ring racing snaffle

❚ ABOVE
butterfly bit

Training and Showing Bits

Some bits are specifically designed for training young horses and for leading and showing horses in-hand.

The **chifney**, also known as an **anti-rearing bit**, consists of a ring which sits in the horse's mouth and is attached to a separate headstall. It is often used when leading stallions and racehorses in the parade ring.

The **Tattersall ring bit**, similar to the chifney, is useful for leading boisterous youngsters. The bit is held in place by a headstall which is attached to the two metal loops on either side. The lead rope is attached to the rear of the ring.

Mouthing or **breaking bits** are designed to encourage young horses to play with the mouthpiece. They can have a single or unjointed mouthpiece and feature small metal "keys" in the centre of the mouthpiece with which the young horse plays.

The **horseshoe stallion bridoon**, which looks similar to the **overcheck bridoon**, is designed for showing stallions in-hand.

■ RIGHT
Top to bottom: **chifney;**
Tattersall ring bit;
horseshoe stallion
bridoon; overcheck
bridoon

■ ABOVE
A Thoroughbred yearling with a Tattersall ring bit
fitted to a leather headcollar.

BIT MATERIALS

Bits are available in a wide variety of metals, alloys and synthetic materials. The following materials are listed in order of common usage.
Stainless steel is strong and easy to clean. Steel is the most popular choice of bit material. One of the disadvantages of steel is that it is a "cold" metal which does not encourage salivation.
Rubber is used to cover metal bits to soften their action. However, rubber is not particularly hardwearing and is easily chewed.
Vulcanite or vulcanized rubber is harder wearing than rubber but heavier and not as flexible.
Polyurethane and **nylon** bits are flexible if unjointed. These materials are also used to cover jointed metal bits. A mouthpiece using polyurethane or nylon can be very mild in action and often has an

copper alloy

vulcanite

happy mouth

rubber

copper and steel

apple scent to make it more appealing to horses.
Copper mouthpieces warm up to the horse's body temperature more quickly than steel but are less hardwearing. They are designed to encourage horses with dry mouths to salivate.
Copper alloy bits are designed to combine the qualities of copper with the strength of stainless steel. Manufacturers claim that they improve the contact between the rider's hands and the horse.
Brass alloy bits are claimed to have the same qualities as copper. They are a combination of brass with silicon and aluminium.
Sweet iron mouthpieces rust very quickly when allowed to get wet, thereby encouraging the horse to salivate.

nathe

stainless steel

brass alloy

sweet iron

Curb Chains and Lip Straps

Curb bits and pelhams should always be fitted with a curb chain or strap. The curb chain brings pressure on the horse's curb groove. The chain or strap itself should be fitted so that it is brought into action when the shank of the curb bit is at an angle of 45 degrees.

The **Western leather curb strap** is used with a Western curb bit. The **single-link curb chain** is light in weight but, because of its design, can pinch the horse's skin; the **double-link curb chain** is preferable to the single-link type as it is less likely to do this. A **leather curb chain** is designed to be fitted to an English curb bit. The **elasticated curb chain**, like the leather curb chain, has a milder action than the metal type. The **rubber-covered chain** is more comfortable for the horse than an uncovered curb chain, and has a milder action on the curb groove.

All English curb straps or chains should be fitted with a fly ring through which a **lip strap** passes. The strap, attached to either side of the curb bit or pelham, helps to keep the curb chain in place.

Fulmer keepers are small leather straps which are fitted to the cheekpieces of a snaffle bridle. They are used to prevent the upper cheekpiece of a full-cheek snaffle from tipping forward. They also help to keep the bit raised in the horse's mouth, preventing the horse from getting his tongue over the bit.

Leather pelham roundings can be fitted to pelhams and certain types of gag bit when only one set of reins is used.

❙ ABOVE
Western curb strap

❙ ABOVE
double-link chain

❙ ABOVE
single-link chain

❙ ABOVE
leather curb chain

❙ ABOVE
elasticated curb chain

❙ ABOVE
rubber-covered chain

❙ RIGHT
Lip strap fitted to
a Weymouth bit.

Nosebands

Nosebands are available in a variety of designs, from those chosen purely for aesthetic reasons, to corrective nosebands which offer more control, acting in conjunction with the bit to increase the strength of the bit action or to prevent the horse evading it.

The **cavesson** is the simplest noseband design available. It is the only type of noseband to use with a double bridle and can also be used with a standing martingale. When fitted correctly, it should have little or no action on the horse's head. The cavesson should be fitted loosely enough to allow room for two fingers under the noseband.

Rope cavessons are much more severe in action than leather ones and are more commonly seen on polo ponies or strong show jumpers. The **continental** or **cinchback cavesson** is designed to be fitted

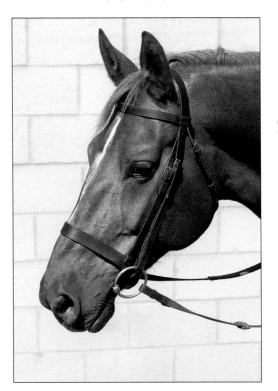

▌ LEFT
cavesson noseband

▌ BELOW
continental cavesson

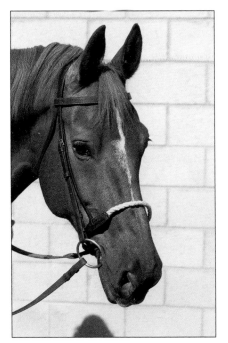

▌ LEFT
rope cavesson
noseband

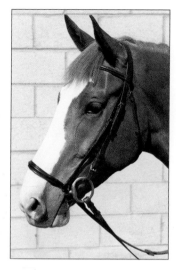

more tightly than a traditional cavesson to discourage the horse from opening his mouth. It can be used with a double bridle and for this reason is often used for dressage or showing.

The **dropped noseband** is fitted with the back strap passing below the bit. It is designed to prevent the horse from opening his mouth and evading the bit. The dropped noseband (when fitted correctly) can increase pressure on the horse's poll as well as on the nose and lower jaw. The dropped noseband should not be used if a standing martingale is fitted. Take care not to fit it below the base of the nasal bone as this can restrict the horse's breathing.

The **flash** is based on the cavesson noseband but has an additional strap which is fitted below the bit. It was originally developed for riders who wanted a noseband which closed the mouth like a dropped noseband, but which could be used alongside a standing martingale. The flash noseband is fitted slightly higher and tighter than the cavesson. Attachments are available which can transform an ordinary cavesson into a flash noseband.

The **Grakle** or **figure-of-eight** takes its name from the eponymous winner of the British 1931 Grand National steeplechase. The Grakle should be fitted snugly so that the top strap goes around the horse's jaws above the bit (resting just below the facial

bone) while the lower strap passes below the bit, keeping the mouth closed. The Grakle puts pressure on the horse's nose (where the straps cross) and helps to stop the horse from crossing his jaws.

Take care that the central point does not lie below the nasal bone as this will cause discomfort to the horse. There should be a short strap fitted at the back of the noseband to keep the straps in place.

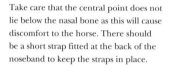

▮ ABOVE
Left to right:
dropped noseband;
flash noseband;
Grakle or figure-of-
eight noseband

▮ LEFT
Mexican Grakle

■ BELOW
Australian cheeker

■ RIGHT
sheepskin noseband

The **Mexican** or **high-ring Grakle** is fitted higher than a normal Grakle, above the cheek bones. It sits higher up the face and is thought to be more effective at preventing the horse crossing his jaws.

The **Kineton** or **Puckle noseband** is a severe noseband which derives its name from its designer, a Mr Puckle of Kineton. Metal loops pass under the bit so that when a contact is taken up, strong pressure is brought to bear on both the nose and the bit, encouraging the horse to lower his head. As with the dropped noseband, take care not to fit it too low.

The **sheepskin noseband**, often used on racehorses, is basically a cavesson noseband covered with a sheepskin sleeve. It encourages the horse to lower his head, which he must do if he is to see over the noseband.

The **Australian cheeker** is a rubber attachment which fastens to the headstall of the bridle and either side of a snaffle bit. It helps to keep the bit raised in the mouth, preventing the horse from getting his tongue over it. It is thought that being able to see the central strap encourages the horse to back off the bit.

The **controller** or **combination noseband** combines the action of a dropped and a Grakle noseband. The two straps help to keep the horse's mouth closed and discourage him from opening his mouth. The front strap is adjustable and is fitted like a dropped noseband. For very strong horses, the front strap can be reinforced with a strip of metal.

■ BELOW LEFT
Kineton noseband

■ BELOW RIGHT
controller noseband

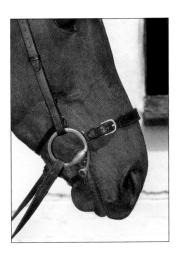

Reins

The reins provide the vital line of communication between your hands and the bit in the horse's mouth.

Plain leather reins are very smart and make an ideal choice for showing. They are often used with double bridles as they are not bulky. A thicker rein is fitted to the bridoon with a thinner rein used for the curb. A disadvantage of plain leather reins is that they can be slippery, especially if allowed to get wet. **Plain leather dressage reins** incorporate small leather "stops" which help to improve grip.

Laced leather reins have thin strips of leather laced through them to improve grip. **Plaited (braided) leather reins** are easy to grip but are more expensive than laced reins and with use they will stretch.

Rubber-covered reins are the popular choice for everyday riding because of their durability. They are very easy to grip, even when wet, and for this reason are often used for racing, eventing and general riding. **Half-rubber reins** are less slippery than plain leather ones, and are more attractive and less cumbersome than rubber-covered reins. **Continental reins** are made of webbing with leather stops to improve grip. **Rubberized webbing reins** are lightweight and incorporate rubber for improved grip.

Plaited (braided) cotton reins are light in weight and reasonably easy to grip. **Plaited (braided) nylon reins** are slightly cheaper than plaited cotton reins, but can be very slippery and will stretch easily. **Western reins** are traditionally ridden split, without being secured at the end with a buckle, to prevent the horse catching his foot if the reins trail on the ground once the rider has dismounted.

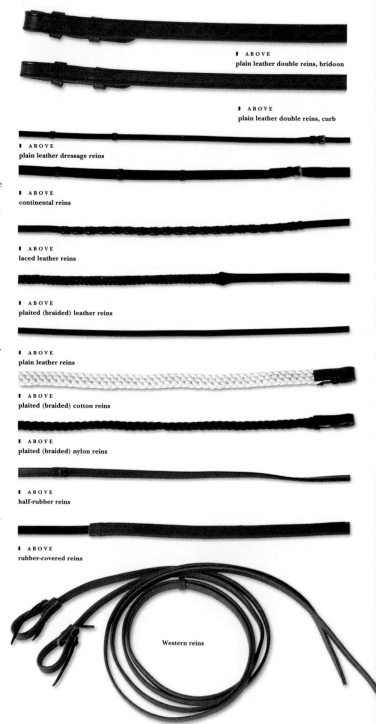

▮ ABOVE
plain leather double reins, bridoon

▮ ABOVE
plain leather double reins, curb

▮ ABOVE
plain leather dressage reins

▮ ABOVE
continental reins

▮ ABOVE
laced leather reins

▮ ABOVE
plaited (braided) leather reins

▮ ABOVE
plain leather reins

▮ ABOVE
plaited (braided) cotton reins

▮ ABOVE
plaited (braided) nylon reins

▮ ABOVE
half-rubber reins

▮ ABOVE
rubber-covered reins

Western reins

Rein Attachments

There are a number of ways in which reins can be attached to the bridle, depending on the reason the horse is being tacked up. For instance in showing classes, where appearance is of the utmost importance, reins will often be stitched on to the bit.

Although this makes changing the bit difficult, it does look much neater than billets (stud hooks) or buckles.

Billets are small metal hooks which fasten into a small hole in the rein to attach it to the bridle. The billet and billet hole should be checked regularly for wear and tear. **Buckles** are a secure way of attaching reins but can look bulky. Western reins are attached to the bit by **hide thongs**. **Loops** are a less secure method of fastening reins than buckles.

❙ BELOW
looped fastening reins

❙ BELOW
buckle fastening on synthetic reins

❙ BELOW
Western reins

❙ BELOW
leather reins with buckle fastening

Browbands

The browband helps to keep the bridle in position on the horse's head. It is very important that the browband is fitted correctly as a browband fitted too loosely looks untidy and may not be effective in preventing the bridle from slipping back. If fitted too tightly, the browband can pinch the horse's ears, thereby forcing him to shake his head. Available in a wide range of designs, browbands are always highly decorative.

The **plain browband** is ideal for horses with heavier, coarser heads. **Padded browbands** feature a raised central section, which suits larger warmblood heads. A raised strip of coloured **plaited (braided) leather** can add contrast to an otherwise plain bridle. **Velvet-covered browbands** are available in a wide choice of colours and can be selected to match your outfit. They are popular for showing hacks and children's ponies. A delicate browband, the **plaited (braided) Arab**, is specially designed to suit the finer features of the Arab horse. **Clincher browbands** have studs (clinchers) in silver or brass. They come in all sorts of decorative designs which feature metal bobbles and small, mirrored strips. **Diamanté browbands** are popular for horses competing indoors where the light catches the stones. The **chain browband** is best suited to horses or ponies with extremely fine heads. The **bit motif browband** incorporates a gilt snaffle design. **Western browbands** can be very simple in design, with little or no ornamentation, although highly decorative browbands with silver detailing are often used for showing or parades. Not all Western bridles feature browbands: the one ear and split ear bridles do not require a browband to keep them in place.

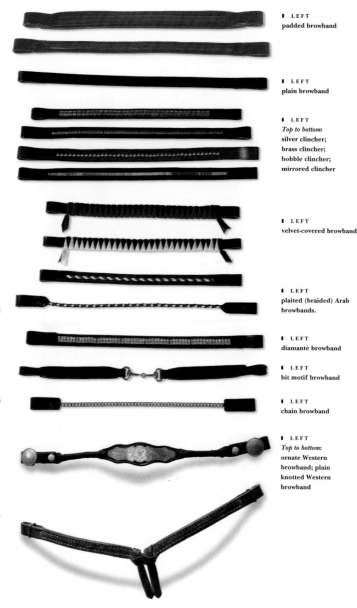

■ LEFT
padded browband

■ LEFT
plain browband

■ LEFT
Top to bottom:
silver clincher;
brass clincher;
bobble clincher;
mirrored clincher

■ LEFT
velvet-covered browband

■ LEFT
plaited (braided) Arab
browbands.

■ LEFT
diamanté browband

■ LEFT
bit motif browband

■ LEFT
chain browband

■ LEFT
Top to bottom:
ornate Western
browband; plain
knotted Western
browband

Bridle Accessories

There is a range of items which can be fitted to the horse's bridle or halter. Many of these pieces are corrective items designed to discourage the horse from a bad habit, while some are aids to improve his comfort.

▌ RIGHT
Bit guards are rubber disks which can be fitted to loose-ring bits to prevent them from pinching the horse's lips. They also help to keep the bit positioned centrally in the horse's mouth.

▌ BELOW
The pricker pad is a leather pad with sharp bristles. It is fitted to one side of the bit against the side of the horse's face to discourage the horse from leaning to one side.

▌ ABOVE
Rein stops should always be fitted when a martingale is used. They stop the martingale rings slipping down towards the bit and getting stuck.

▌ ABOVE
Blinkers are mainly used on racehorses. They block the horse's view to either side, helping him to concentrate and thus improve his racing performance.

▌ ABOVE
A face net is a fine mesh net which is fitted over the horse's head. It can help protect the horse from flies when he is turned out in the field.

▌ RIGHT
Martingale stops are fitted to running and standing martingales to stop the central strap slipping through the chestpiece.

▌ RIGHT
The tongue guard is a rubber attachment which fastens to the bit. It is used to prevent the horse getting his tongue over the bit.

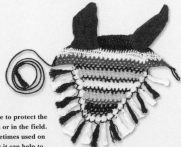

▌ ABOVE AND RIGHT
Fly fringes are attached to the bridle to protect the horse's face from flies when ridden or in the field. The type with earpieces is also sometimes used on show jumpers competing indoors as it can help to muffle spectator noise. A simpler fly fringe can be fitted to the horse's headcollar to protect him from flies when turned out in the field.

Putting on a Bridle

1 Stand on the near (left) side of the horse and hold the headpiece (crownpiece) of the bridle in your right hand. Place your left hand (holding the bit) under the horse's muzzle.

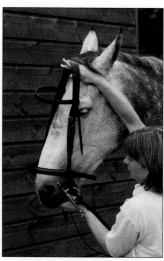

2 Press your thumb firmly but gently against the bars of the horse's mouth to encourage him to open his mouth.

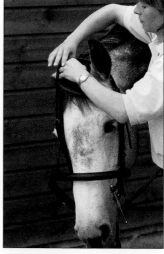

3 Guide the bit gently into the horse's mouth, taking care not to bang it against his teeth. Draw the bridle up with the right hand and, using the left hand, guide the left and then the right ear under the headpiece of the bridle.

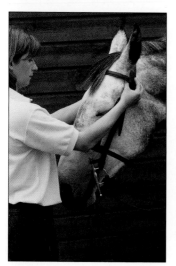

4 Separate the mane under the headpiece (a small section of mane, called a bridle path, can be clipped from this area) and bring the forelock out over the browband.

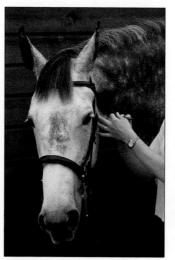

5 Fasten the throatlatch. It should be loose enough to allow you to fit four fingers between the throatlatch and the horse's cheeks.

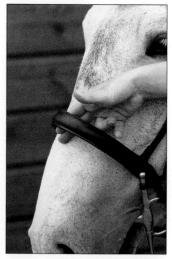

6 Fasten the noseband (in this case a cavesson) so that it passes underneath the cheekpieces of the bridle. It should be loose enough to allow you to place two fingers underneath the noseband.

CLEANING THE BRIDLE

Bridle Care

A leather bridle should be cleaned regularly to keep it in top condition and to prolong its life. Remove sweat and grime every time the bridle is used and once a week dismantle it completely for a thorough cleaning. A synthetic bridle can be simply wiped down with a damp cloth or immersed in water. Check the stitching and billets (stud hooks) regularly, paying particular attention to where the bit is attached to the bridle at the reins and the cheekpieces.

1 Hang the bridle from a suitable hook, undoing all the straps from their keepers.

2 Wipe the bridle down with a damp sponge to remove dirt and grease.

3 Use a clean sponge to rub in lightly moistened saddle soap.

4 Wipe the bit, or rinse it under running water. Do this each time it has been used to prevent a build-up of saliva and food.

A correctly put up bridle. Cross the throatlatch over the front of the bridle, loop up the reins and fasten the noseband around it.

❙ LEFT
Jockeys will often tie a knot at the end of the reins. This is a safety measure in case the buckle joining the reins were to break during the race.

Training Aids
and Gadgets

There is a saying that gadgets and training aids are fine in the
hands of experts but that experts have no need for them. This may
apply in an ideal world but every horseman or woman, however
expert, will encounter problems when schooling and training
horses and may occasionally need additional help in the form of
an aid or a gadget.

A training aid is a piece of equipment used to develop a
well-schooled, obedient horse to improve his performance, while
a gadget is a piece of equipment which prevents or restrains an
aspect of the horse's behaviour which makes him dangerous or
difficult to ride.

A degree of skill is required when using training aids or gadgets.
The equipment must be fitted correctly, and you must be aware of
its strength and severity. Only use it when it is specifically required,
never as a matter of course. Training aids and gadgets in the
wrong hands can damage the horse physically and psychologically.

▮ OPPOSITE
A rider schooling on
the flat to encourage
obedience and
suppleness.

▮ LEFT
A leather lungeing
cavesson.

Martingales

Martingales are designed to assist the bridle in controlling the horse. They prevent the horse from raising his head beyond the point at which the rider can control him.

The **running martingale** consists of a neck strap and a second strap which is attached to the girth and passes between the horse's front legs before dividing into two pieces. At the end of each of these straps is a small metal ring through which the reins pass. **Rein stops** should be fitted to the reins, below the bit, to prevent the martingale rings from getting caught on the bit. When the horse carries his head in the correct position no pressure is felt. However, when he raises his head above a certain point, the martingale restricts the movement of the reins which in turn causes the bit to bear down on the bars of the horse's mouth. The running martingale should be fitted so that the rings are in line with the withers to prevent it putting any pressure on the

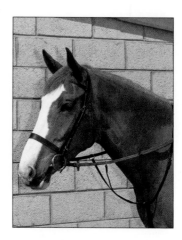

▌ ABOVE
running martingale

▌ BELOW LEFT
combined breastplate and martingale

▌ BELOW RIGHT
bib martingale

reins when the horse's head is held in the correct position. It should not be used in conjunction with a curb bit.

The **bib martingale** is a variation on the running martingale. The two straps of the martingale are joined by a triangle of leather. This is to prevent an excitable horse from getting caught up in the straps; the design is often used on racehorses.

The **combined breastplate and martingale** is a traditional heavyweight hunting-style breastplate used to stop the saddle from slipping back. The breastplate has a central ring to which a running martingale attachment is fixed.

The **standing martingale** has a single strap which is attached to the girth, passes between the horse's front legs and is fixed to the back of the noseband (a cavesson or the cavesson part of a flash noseband). Like the running martingale, it has a neck strap. When correctly fitted it should be possible to push the martingale strap up into the horse's gullet.

A **rubber martingale stop** should always be fitted to running and standing martingales to stop the martingale from slipping through the neck strap, which could result in the horse getting a foot caught in the straps.

The **Market Harborough** consists of a leather strap attached to the girth, which passes between the horse's front legs before dividing into two straps with a clip at each end. These straps pass through the bit rings and are clipped on to one of a series of rings on the side of the reins. Like the running martingale, the Market Harborough will only put pressure on the bit (and as a consequence on the bars of the horse's mouth) if the horse brings his head up beyond a certain point. The Market Harborough should only be used with an ordinary snaffle.

The **Irish martingale**, unlike other martingales, has no direct action on the horse's head carriage. It consists of a short piece of leather with a ring at either end through which the reins pass. The Irish martingale is used to prevent the reins from being pulled over the horse's head in the event of a fall. It can also be used for horses who have a habit of suddenly tossing their heads in the air – "star gazers" – resulting in the reins being thrown over their heads.

Training Reins

Training reins are used when schooling the horse to help him develop the correct musculature for ridden work, or as a corrective aid to encourage the horse to carry himself well.

Running reins, also known as **draw reins**, are long pieces of leather or webbing with a loop at each end which fit around either side of the girth; the reins pass through the bit rings (from the inside to the outside) and up to the rider's hands. Running reins encourage the horse to lower his head, bringing it towards the vertical to promote the correct development of his back muscles. Running reins should only be used with an ordinary snaffle bridle to which an independent set of reins is also attached, and the rider must be quick to release the pressure on the running reins when the horse lowers his head. It is important that the horse is ridden forwards or there is a danger that he will become over-bent (with his head held behind the vertical).

A more severe method of fitting running reins is to attach them to the

Running reins attached to either side of the girth.

girth at the chest before passing them through the front legs up to the bit and back to the rider's hands. Fitted in this way the running reins (more correctly referred to as draw reins) impart a stronger leverage action on the horse's head.

An **overcheck rein** has a centre buckle and passes over the horse's poll, through the bit rings to the rider's hands. Overcheck reins will encourage the horse to raise his head by raising the bit in his mouth, rather like a gag snaffle.

Attach running reins at the chest for more control.

The **De Gogue schooling system** is used for ridden work or lungeing. A strap from the girth passes between the horse's legs and divides into two cord straps. A piece of leather with pulleys on either side is fixed to the headpiece of the bridle. The cord straps go over the pulleys and down to the bit. For ridden work, short reins can be attached to the straps (with a second independent set of reins also fitted). For lungeing, the cords pass through the bit rings and clip on to the chest strap.

The De Gogue schooling system for lungeing or ridden work.

The Chambon system for lungeing or loose schooling only.

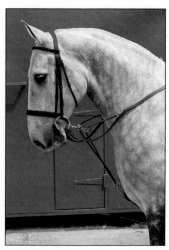
The Abbot Davies balancing rein.

▮ LEFT
Two ways of attaching the
elastic training rein.

▮ BELOW
The Pessoa training
system.

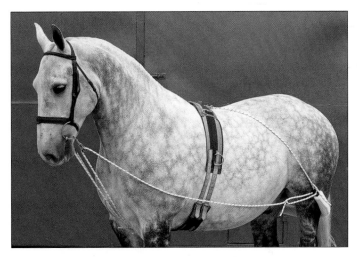

The **Chambon** is a schooling system consisting of a poll pad fitted over the top of the horse's head, to which pulleys are attached on either side. A strap is attached to the lungeing roller which passes up between the horse's front legs before dividing into two cords. The two cords fit over the pulleys and are clipped on to the bit rings. The Chambon encourages the horse to lower his head and neck and round his back, which in turn encourages engagement of the hindquarters. The Chambon can be used on horses which are being loose-schooled but is not designed to be ridden in.

The **Abbot Davies balancing rein** encourages the horse to develop the muscles of his back and hindquarters by raising his neck at its base. A combined system of pulleys and straps will prevent the horse leaning. It can be fitted from tail to mouth but more commonly, or in the latter stages of training, it is fitted from girth to mouth or mouth to ears.

The **Harbridge** aims to encourage the horse to work correctly by discouraging leaning, enhancing self-carriage and generally stimulating softness in the horse's back. It is not dissimilar in appearance to a running martingale. A strap attached to the girth passes through the horse's front legs and divides

into two pieces of elastic which are clipped on to the bit rings. It should be used for flat work only, and is not suitable for schooling over jumps.

The **Schoolmasta training aid** is designed for horses which lean on the bit or have a tendency to over-bend and carry their heads behind the vertical. The system works independently of the rider's hands: straps clipped on to either side of the bit are attached to a pulley fitted to a special numnah, and this helps to correct the horse's posture.

The **elastic training rein** fits over the horse's poll, passes through the rings and clips on to the girth at the side or at the chest. The rein is designed to promote self-carriage without putting pressure on the horse's mouth.

The **Pessoa training system** aims to give the horse a rounded outline. It consists of a roller and pulleys attached from the roller to the bit rings, and to a strap passed round the hindquarters. As with all training equipment, skill and experience are needed for it to be used successfully.

The **Harbridge** has two elasticated straps which clip on to the bit.

The **Schoolmasta** training aid is used in conjunction with a specially adapted numnah.

Lungeing and Long Reining

Lungeing is a method of exercising or training the horse from a single long rein. The horse is worked in a circle, at a distance of 20m/66ft from the handler, in both directions and in walk, trot and canter.

The **lunge cavesson** is an essential piece of lungeing equipment. It is fitted over a bridle if side reins are to be used. A lunge line is attached to the central ring on the noseband. The cavesson should fit snugly so that it does not slip when in use.

Lungeing and **breaking rollers** are necessary when side reins or long lines are used. In the examples shown here, the top roller has large rings through which long-reining lines are fitted. Side reins can be attached to the smaller D rings. A crupper prevents the roller slipping forward; a breastgirth keeps it from slipping back. Lungeing the horse with side reins fitted

I LEFT AND BELOW
Shown here are two examples of a lunge cavesson, in leather (*left*) and webbing (*below*).

I BELOW
Top to bottom: Leather breaking roller, leather lunge roller and web lunge roller.

enables the handler to influence the horse's outline and general way of going by containing impulsion. Working the horse on long lines enables the trainer to teach the young horse to respond to the feel of reins before a rider is introduced.

The **Elwyn Hartley-Edwards breaking roller** is a webbing and leather roller designed specifically for training the young horse. It features a built-in crupper to prevent the roller from being pulled forwards as the horse is worked.

Side reins are attached to the roller and clip on to the bit rings to encourage the horse to work in a correct outline. There is some debate as to whether elasticated or non-elasticated types are better. Some trainers feel that a rein that "gives" is better than a fixed type, while others suggest that elasticated reins can encourage the horse to evade the contact of the reins.

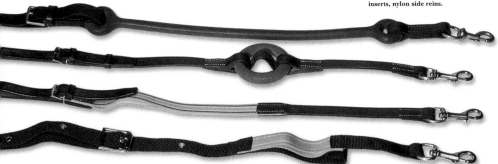

■ BELOW
Top to bottom: Rubber side reins,
continental pattern side reins,
leather side reins with elastic
inserts, nylon side reins.

Continental pattern side reins in
leather have rubber inserts which allow
the reins to "give" as the horse moves.
Leather side reins are available, many
with elastic inserts. Leather side reins
can be costly but if well cared for they
will last longer than synthetic ones. **Nylon
side reins**, with or without elastic inserts,
are a cheaper alternative.

The **lunge line**, available in cord or
webbing, is attached to the central ring
on the lunge cavesson by means of a
spring clip or a buckled strap. The lunge
line enables the handler to control and
guide the horse around a circle.

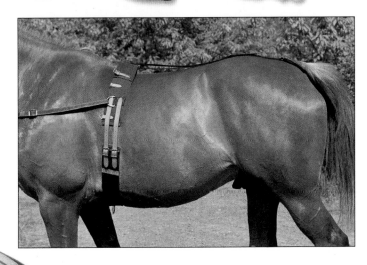

■ ABOVE
The Elwyn Hartley-Edwards breaking
roller shown fitted with side reins
and a crupper.

■ LEFT
lunge lines

65

LUNGEING CAVESSON FITTED OVER A BRIDLE

The cavesson has been fitted over a bridle with the noseband removed. The reins have been twisted and looped through the throatlatch to prevent the horse accidentally getting caught in them. The side reins are attached to the bit rings: these should only be attached when the horse is being lunged. Start with the side reins fitted loosely and adjust them as the horse warms up.

HORSE TACKED UP FOR LUNGEING

Lungeing roller fitted with a breastplate.

USING A SADDLE INSTEAD OF A ROLLER

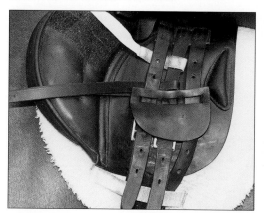

1 Side reins can be fitted to the girth straps on a saddle instead of the roller. They are useful if you plan to ride the horse after it has been lunged or if the horse is being lunged with a rider on board. The side reins pass round the second girth strap and under the first. This will prevent them from slipping down.

2 The stirrups can be removed from the saddle or, if the horse is to be ridden, they can be held securely in place by looping the stirrup leather around the stirrup and securing it with the spare end.

Lead Reins and Ropes

Lead reins and ropes are essential items of equipment when handling horses.

Lead ropes are inexpensive and sturdy, and are the practical choice for everyday use. They are clipped on to the horse's headcollar or halter so that he can be secured when travelling, or when being groomed or tacked up. Cotton and plaited (braided) nylon lead ropes come in a variety of colours: choose one to match your horse's headcollar.

When securing a horse with a lead rope, always use a quick release knot to allow the horse to be untied quickly in an emergency. Tying a horse directly to a fixed object, such as a gate or metal tie ring, can risk injuring him if he decides to pull back suddenly. Instead, attach the rope to the fixed object with a loop of bailing twine. If the horse pulls back suddenly, the twine will break and the horse will be released unhurt.

Leather and **webbing lead reins** are very smart and are commonly used for showing horses in-hand. The leather type has a double chain attachment called a **Newmarket chain**, which clips on to either bit ring and gives the handler greater control over the horse. The webbing lead rein is popular for showing and attaches directly to the headcollar or halter.

■ BELOW
plaited (braided) nylon
lead rope

■ BELOW
cotton lead rope

■ BELOW
webbing (*top*) and leather
lead reins

Headcollars and Halters

Headcollars and halters are indispensable items of tack which are used to lead horses in-hand or to secure them when travelling or in the stable. Some are also designed to control or restrain horses.

The best-quality **leather headcollars** are made from English leather and, like all good-quality leather tack, they will last for years if well cared for. As an extra feature, you can attach a brass plate engraved with your horse's name.

Synthetic headcollars are ideal for everyday use. They are extremely strong, although this can be a problem – if the horse is turned out in one and gets caught on a branch, gate or fence, the synthetic headcollar will not break easily. The **synthetic rope halter** is made of strong nylon cord and fastens simply by tying. **Rope halters** are commonly used for showing young stock in-hand.

The **Controller headcollar** can be used for horses with a tendency to pull when led in-hand. The headcollar is designed to apply pressure on the nose when the horse pulls against the handler.

The **"Be-Nice"** halter, popularized by the American trainer, Monty Roberts, will train the horse to be led in-hand. The halter tightens around the horse's head and applies pressure to the poll when the horse resists being led. It should never be used to secure the horse.

The decorative **Western show halter** is made from leather with engraved silver detailing. The **in-hand bridle** is halfway between a bridle and a headcollar. It has short leather straps to which a bit is fitted and is used, as its name implies, for showing horses in-hand. The **rolled Arab slip** is a delicate halter which will enhance the fineness of the Arab head in in-hand showing classes. The **foal slip** is designed as a first headcollar for young foals. The short strap which hangs down is used instead of a separate lead rope.

A leather headcollar makes a very smart piece of equipment. A brass plate engraved with the horse's name can be fitted as an extra feature.

The synthetic headcollar is strong, durable and easy to care for. It is available in many colours and is a popular choice for children's ponies.

The unusual design of the synthetic rope halter means that it can be fastened without buckles.

The simple rope halter is popular for showing young horses in-hand.

▌ ABOVE LEFT
Controller headcollar

▌ ABOVE MIDDLE
"Be-Nice" halter

▌ ABOVE RIGHT
Western show halter

▌ LEFT AND
RIGHT
foal slip

▌ ABOVE LEFT
in-hand bridle

▌ BELOW LEFT
rolled Arab slip

Clothing and Equipment

The ridden horse needs a variety of clothing and equipment to keep him warm, clean and dry, and to protect him from injury. Rugs are a necessity for clipped horses and for fine-skinned, hot-blooded types such as Thoroughbreds. Modern rugs are lighter in weight than their predecessors, making them more comfortable for horses to wear and easier to clean. They are also more effective at keeping the horse warm, dry, cool or clean. There is always a risk that a horse may be injured during exercise or when he is competing or travelling to and from shows. To minimize the risk there is a range of equipment and clothing available to protect him literally from top to tail. Grooming equipment is an essential part of the horse owner's kit. Whether your horse lives out or is stabled, regular grooming will help maintain his health by encouraging good circulation, removing dirt and dead skin and generally improving his appearance. Keeping the horse's coat clean will also help to keep the tack itself clean.

▮ OPPOSITE
Horses need extra protection from the potential hazards of road travel.

▮ LEFT
felt covering boots

Turnout and Stable Rugs

TURNOUT RUGS

Turnout rugs are used to keep the horse warm and dry when turned out in the field. Turnout rugs are made from tough synthetic fabrics. Modern turnout rugs incorporate state-of-the-art breathable materials which are highly water- and windproof but still allow moisture to pass from the horse's body through the rug, preventing the horse from getting overheated.

The **New Zealand turnout rug** is a heavyweight canvas turnout rug, so-called because it was first developed in New Zealand. The self-righting type has breast and leg straps which help the rug to stay in place, whatever the horse gets up to.

The **Wug** and **Gladiator turnout rugs** are made from synthetic material. Both feature an extended neck which helps to keep the horse warm and dry.

❚ LEFT
The Gladiator turnout rug features a useful neck cover.

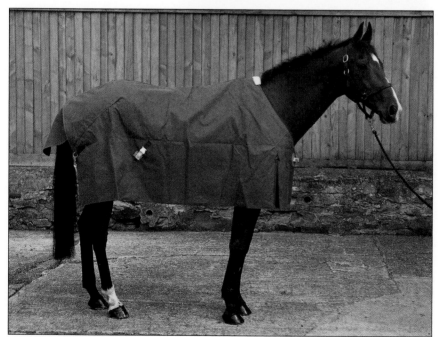

❚ LEFT
The New Zealand rug is a heavyweight proofed canvas turnout rug.

■ BELOW
The synthetic stable
rug can be used as a
day or night rug.

■ RIGHT
quilted foal rug

STABLE RUGS

Stable rugs keep the horse clean and
warm in the stable. The models available
range from lightweight cotton rugs for
summer to thick quilted rugs for winter.

Melton day rugs are made of wool
and are available in a range of colours.
A woollen rug will keep the horse warm
but it can be heavy and less breathable
than modern fabrics, and is more
difficult to clean. Woollen rugs can be
personalized with the owner's initials or
a sponsor's logo.

The **synthetic stable rug** is a modern
alternative to the traditional woollen rug.
New fabric technology means that stable
rugs can be both lightweight and warm,
allowing any sweat from the horse's body
to pass through the fabric. Because they
are easy to wash, synthetic stable rugs also
work well as night rugs.

Under rugs (blanket liners), available
in different thicknesses, are designed to
be fitted under a horse's stable rug to
provide extra warmth during the cold
winter months. Extra warmth may also
be provided by a **horse blanket** fitted
under a stable or night rug.

Jute rugs, traditionally used as night
rugs, have a natural fibre outer layer and
a blanket lining. Their main disadvantage
is that they are very heavy.

■ RIGHT
The woollen Melton
day rug is effective
at keeping the horse
warm, but is heavier
than rugs made from
synthetic fabrics.

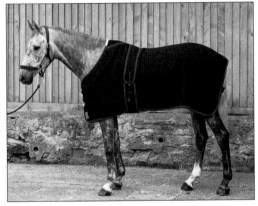

■ BELOW
The jute rug is a
natural fibre rug
traditionally used
as a night rug.

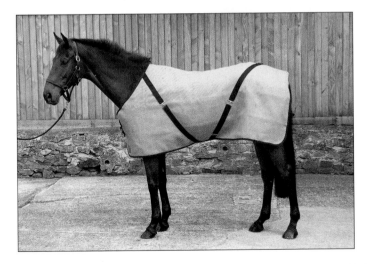

Sheets and Coolers

SHEETS

Sheets are made from lighter materials than turnout or stable rugs. A sheet can be used either in the summer months when the temperatures are higher, or immediately before or after exercise.

Summer (stable) sheets, made from linen or cotton, are lightweight rugs used to help keep the stabled horse clean.

Paddock sheets are shaped rugs in cotton or wool, so-called because they are used to keep racehorses warm while being paraded in the paddock before the race. The paddock rug is held in place with a surcingle and breastgirth. It can double as an exercise sheet, also called a half-sheet or quarter-sheet, to keep the racehorse's hindquarters warm during early morning exercise on the gallops.

Many exercise sheets are designed to keep the horse warm and dry while active, and are particularly useful for clipped horses. The synthetic polypropylene fabric used for the **wicking exercise sheet** will only allow moisture to pass through if the horse begins to sweat. This type of exercise sheet is worn under the saddle.

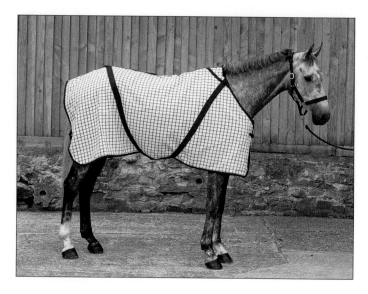

▮ BELOW
paddock sheet

COOLERS

Coolers are multi-purpose rugs, often incorporating the latest developments in fabric technology. They allow the horse to dry off quickly after exercise or bathing without the risk of catching a chill because of a wicking effect which allows moisture to pass from the horse's body through the fabric. Cooler rugs are ideal for those horses with a tendency to sweat profusely when travelling.

The non-absorbent breathable fabric of the **Coolmasta rug** makes it suitable for use as an anti-sweat rug, a travelling rug or a stable rug. The polypropylene fabric of the **Universal wicking rug** allows dampness from the horse's body to pass through the rug to prevent chills, as does the **fleece rug**. The **Combi sweat (anti-sweat) rug and fly sheet (scrim)** is a fine-mesh rug. The knit of the cotton fabric creates air pockets which help the horse to dry off quickly. These rugs can be used on a stabled horse under a lightweight summer sheet to speed up the drying process after exercise.

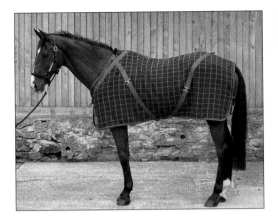

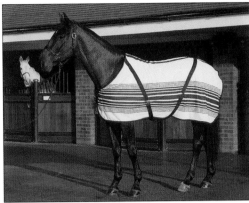

 ABOVE LEFT
Universal wicking rug. A multi-purpose rug which
lets body moisture through the fabric to prevent
the horse catching a chill.

ABOVE RIGHT
Coolmasta synthetic rug. A cooler which is versatile
enough to be used as a summer (stable) sheet,
anti-sweat rug, travel or day rug.

RIGHT
Fleece rug. While moisture evaporates away
through the rug, the fleece fabric ensures that
the horse's body temperature does not drop.

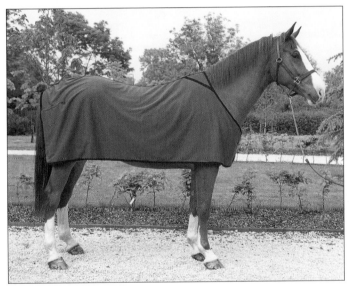

BELOW
Combi sweat (anti-sweat) rug and fly sheet (scrim).
A fine mesh rug which can be used under a summer
sheet to speed up drying.

BELOW RIGHT
Rain sheet. This waterproof rug (cover) will keep
the horse dry at shows and competitions.

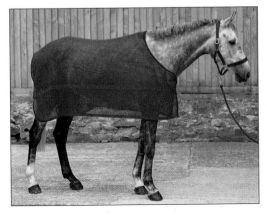

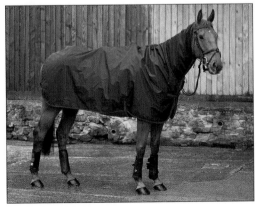

Specialist Sheets and Rugs

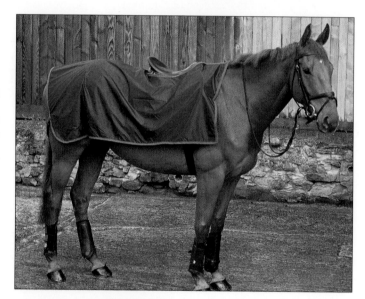

Besides the basic types of rug, an increasing number of rug products are available for more specific needs.

Exercise sheets will keep thin-skinned horses warm and dry during exercise sessions. The **continental waterproof exercise sheet** has a lightweight outer shell with a twill lining and can be fitted over the saddle in wet weather. The **fluorescent exercise sheet** ensures that both horse and rider are easily seen by other road users, and is especially useful for anyone who has to ride on roads at times of poor visibility.

The **rain sheet** is a lightweight synthetic sheet which covers the horse from ears to tail. The sheet will keep the horse dry at competitions and shows but should not be used on horses turned out in the field.

New-born foals do not normally require rugs. However, the **quilted foal rug** can be very useful in helping to keep a sickly foal warm in the stable.

The **rug bib (blanket bib)** is fitted under the rug to prevent it from rubbing the horse's shoulders, leading to sores and bare patches in his coat.

Hoods can be fitted to rugs to provide extra warmth and to help keep the horse clean. The **outdoor hood**, made from a synthetic material, can be fitted to a turnout rug. The **lycra hood** is used in the stable to keep the horse clean.

Chest extenders are panels of fabric with straps which can be buckled on to the horse's existing rug to provide a better fit.

■ ABOVE
A rug bib is fitted
under the rug to
prevent the rug
from rubbing.

■ ABOVE
golden stripe horse blanket

■ BELOW
lycra hood

■ BELOW
under rug

Fitting a Rug

Whatever type of rug you use, it is important that it is fitted correctly. Rugs are often left on for long periods of time and an ill-fitting rug can cause rubbing and discomfort. Rugs are sized according to their length, with the measurement based on the length of the horse taken from the centre of the chest to the tail.

HOW TO PUT ON A RUG

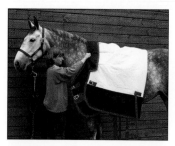 

1 Stand on the near (left) side of the horse. Fold the blanket in half widthways and place it over the horse's neck. Fold the rug back over the horse's hindquarters.

2 Fasten the cross surcingles, but not too tightly: there should be room for the width of a hand between the horse's belly and the straps. These straps should be fastened first so that there is no risk of the rug ending up hanging around the horse's neck, or worse still, his legs.

HOW TO REMOVE A RUG

To remove the rug, undo the leg straps first, then the chest straps and finally the cross surcingles. Fold the front of the rug over the horse's hindquarters and slide off carefully.

3 Next fasten the chest straps: there should be room for a hand's width at the chest.

4 Finally, fasten the leg straps. Fitted correctly, the straps should hang clear of the horse's legs so that they do not rub, but should not be loose enough for the horse to get his leg caught.

▌ RIGHT
Modern turnout rugs allow horses to spend time out in their field whatever the weather. It is important to remember that turned out horses should have their rugs checked at least once a day, as the rug can slip and become uncomfortable for the horse.

Rug Rollers and Surcingles

Most modern stable rugs have surcingles already fitted but separate rollers and surcingles can be used to keep in place those rugs which do not incorporate their own. A separate roller or surcingle is also necessary when more than one rug at a time is worn, to keep them both in place.

Rollers and surcingles should be fitted snugly enough to secure the rug, but they should not be so tight as to be uncomfortable for the horse after long periods of time. Correctly tightened, there should be just enough room to allow four fingers between the roller or surcingle and the rug.

Surcingles used to secure rugs differ significantly from surcingles used to secure saddles, since the needs of the turned out horse and the ridden horse are not the same. The **rug surcingle** is designed for comfort. It is wrapped in protective padding and replaces the buckles and clasps of the saddle surcingle with thick rounded straps, to allow the horse the freedom to sit or roll.

The **elasticated surcingle** fits around the horse's girth. If you are using one of these, it is a good idea to fit a pad over the withers to prevent pressure sores. The **elasticated roller** has padding built in to the area in contact with the withers, as does the **jute surcingle**, which fastens with strong leather straps.

The **anti-cast roller**, made from webbing and leather, has a large metal hoop on the top which prevents the horse from getting cast or wedged when rolling in his stable (stall).

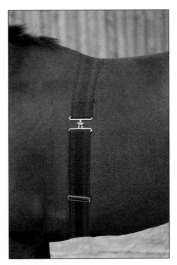

Elasticated surcingle. This type should be used with a pad over the withers to prevent pressure sores.

Elasticated roller. This type has padding built in to protect the withers.

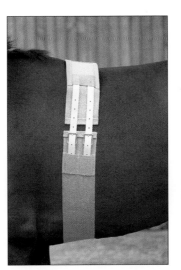

Jute surcingle. This type has built-in padding and fastens with strong leather straps.

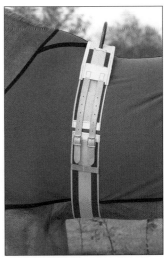

Webbing anti-cast roller. The large metal hoop on the top prevents the horse from getting cast.

Boots

Boots are designed to protect the
horse's legs when travelling, turned
out or being ridden, and a wide choice
is available. Many equestrian activities
place extreme demands on the horse's
legs and protection is needed to prevent
injury. Some horses are also predisposed
conformationally to striking themselves
accidentally while being exercised.

Brushing boots, also referred to
as **splint boots**, have a reinforced pad
along the inside of the boot to prevent
injuries caused when one leg knocks
against the other. The boot should start
just below the knee and finish just below
the fetlock (or ankle) joint. **Hind brushing
boots** are longer than **fore brushing boots**
to protect the hind cannon bone. **Leather
brushing boots** have buckle and strap
fastenings. They are tougher than
synthetic boots but must be looked after
to maintain their condition. **Synthetic
brushing boots** are held in place with
Velcro straps. They are lightweight and
easily washed.

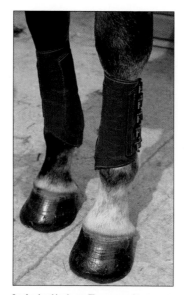

Leather brushing boots. These are used to prevent
injuries inflicted as the horse is being brushed.

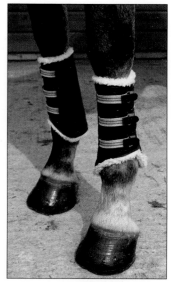

Synthetic brushing boots. These particular boots
are fleece lined to prevent rubbing.

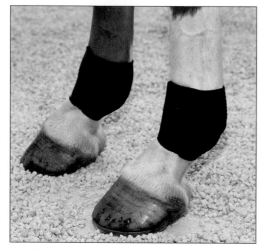

Sesamoid boots. These boots protect the base of the horse's fetlock.

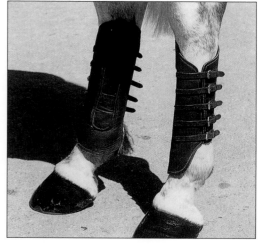

Speedicut boots. These are fitted to the hind legs to prevent injuries if the horse
were to accidentally kick himself while galloping.

■ BELOW
Leather tendon boots protect the tendons which
run down the back of the horse's leg.

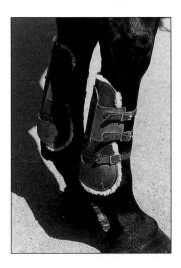

■ BELOW
Synthetic tendon boots are cheaper and easier to
clean than the leather boots.

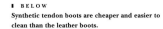

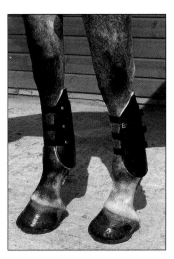

Speedicut boots are fitted to the hind legs and are designed to protect against injuries that occur when one leg strikes another during fast work. When the horse is travelling at high speed, the vulnerable area is the upper part of the leg, hence the boot's extra length.

Tendon boots are designed to protect the tendons which run down the back of the horse's lower foreleg, so are normally open-fronted. The boots should start high enough to protect the tendon and extend low enough to protect the fetlock joint. **Leather tendon boots** have buckle and strap fastenings and may be lined with sheepskin to prevent rubbing. **Synthetic tendon boots** usually have strap and clip fastenings.

Open-fronted boots are popular with show jumpers because they protect the vulnerable part of the horse's leg while still allowing him to feel the poles of the jump.

Sesamoid boots protect the base of the fetlock joint and are often used on racehorses that are trained or run on all-weather or dirt tracks. The base of the fetlock would be damaged if unprotected as it touches the ground as the result of the forces exerted when galloping.

Fetlock boots are shortened versions of brushing boots, fitted to the hindlegs. **Skid boots** are used for Western riding, and are fitted to prevent fetlock injuries which can occur when the horse makes sliding halts.

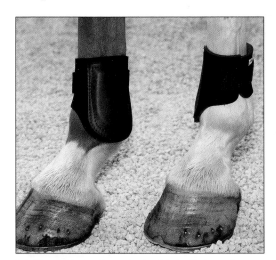

Fetlock boots. These are a shortened version of the brushing boot, and are normally fitted to the hindlegs only.

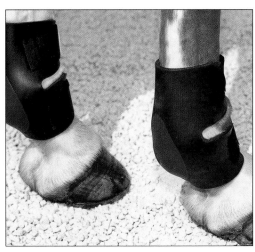

Skid boots. These are fitted to prevent injuries to the fetlock when the horse comes to a sliding halt.

Free knee boots prevent damage to the horse's knees when jumping. Because of their design – they can flip up – they are not suitable for road work or travelling. **Skeleton knee boots** have a lower strap fitted which prevents the pad from flipping up in the event of the horse falling. They are not suitable for jumping as there is a risk that the horse could get a hoof caught in the back strap.

The **coronet ring**, also called an anti-brushing ring, is fitted to one of a pair of legs to prevent brushing injuries. A **sausage boot**, also referred to as a **shoe-boil boot**, is used on stabled horses to prevent injury to the elbow when the horse lies down.

Overreach boots, or **bell boots**, prevent overreach injuries. An overreach is caused by the toe of the hind foot striking into the heel or coronet of the front foot. **Pull-on rubber overreach boots** can be difficult to get on but, once on, stay in place well. A disadvantage of this type of overreach boot is that they can flip up, in which case they will not protect the heel and coronet. **Velcro-fastened rubber overreach boots** are easier to put on and take off. **Petal boots** are less likely to flip up because of their segmented design. They are made up of a series of tough plastic segments or petals which are attached to a strap fitted around the coronet.

Covering boots are felt shoes which fit over the mare's hind feet. They are used on mares being covered, to avoid risking injury to the stallion should the mare try to kick him.

▌ LEFT
Free knee boots. Because of their design, these boots are not suitable for roadwork or travelling.

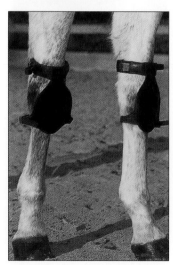

▌ ABOVE
Skeleton knee boots. These have a lower strap fitted which prevents the pad flipping up.

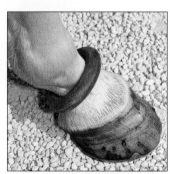

▌ ABOVE
Coronet ring. This is fitted to one leg to prevent brushing injuries.

▌ RIGHT
Sausage boot. These are used on stabled horses to prevent injuries to the elbow.

▮ LEFT
Protection is necessary to guard against the hazards encountered during the cross-country phase of a one-day event. Because the horse is jumping fixed objects, it is vital that his legs are protected with boots or bandages.

▮ ABOVE
Mare's covering boots. These felt shoes are fitted over the mare's hind feet to protect the stallion should she lash out at him.

▮ ABOVE
Velcro-fastened rubber overreach boots. This type is easier to put on and take off than the pull-on variety of overreach boot.

▮ RIGHT
Pull-on rubber overreach boots. These moulded boots will sit securely on the hoof, but they do flip up easily and can offer no protection when this happens.

▮ LEFT
Petal boots are made up of a series of tough plastic segments which are attached to a strap.

EXERCISE BOOTS

Exercise boots, such as brushing boots, are much more convenient to use than exercise bandages (polo wraps) as they are quicker and easier to put on.

▮ BELOW
Skid boots are worn by reining horses to protect the base of the fetlock joint from injury as he comes to a sliding halt.

FITTING BRUSHING BOOTS

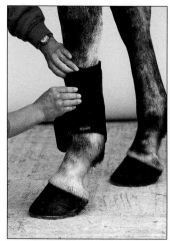

1 Never kneel down when putting on or taking off boots – always crouch so that you can get out of the way quickly should the horse suddenly move. When fitting boots with two straps, fasten the top strap first.

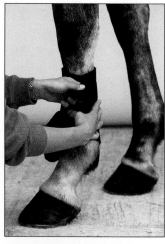

2 On most boots, straps fasten from the front to the back. For boots with more than two straps, fasten the middle strap first, then the top strap and finally the bottom strap or straps.

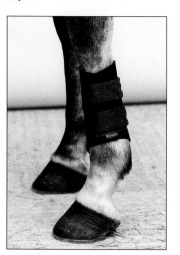

3 Be careful not to over-tighten boots as this is uncomfortable for the horse and can damage the tendons in his lower legs.

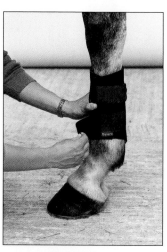

4 When removing boots, undo the bottom strap before unfastening the top one.

THERAPY BOOTS

These boots are designed to keep in place poultices, which are used to draw out dirt from a wound, and otherwise to assist in the treatment of injuries.

Rubber over-shoes fit over the horse's foot. One of these can be used to cover a foot bandage or poultice, or to protect the unshod hoof during ridden work. The **Tenderfoot sox** is used to hold a foot poultice in place.

A **tendon-hosing boot** fitted to the horse's lower leg allows cold water to be trickled down the leg to help reduce swelling caused by stresses, strains or injuries. If something more than a trickle is needed **aqua boots**, covering the entire lower leg and foot, are attached to a compressor which forces water to move around inside, massaging the lower leg.

Magnetic therapy boots are available in various designs. They incorporate thin, flexible magnetic pads which, when placed over the injured area, are said to assist in the repair of muscle, tendon or bone damage.

▮ **LEFT**
rubber over-shoe

▮ **LEFT**
magnetic therapy boots

▮ **BELOW LEFT**
tendon-hosing boot

▮ **BELOW RIGHT**
aqua boots

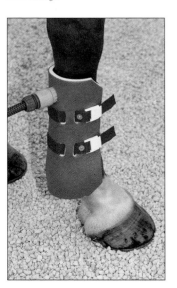

Bandages and Pads

BANDAGES

Like boots, bandages can be used to protect the horse's legs during exercise or travelling as well as for first-aid purposes.

Travelling or **stable bandages** are non-stretch bandages usually made of wool or acrylic and used for warmth and protection. To prevent pressure sores developing on the leg, they should always be used with padding underneath.

Exercise or **tail bandages** are lighter in weight than stable bandages. They are usually slightly elasticated and are held in place with ties. When used to protect the leg during competitions, in particular horse trials, they can be stitched in place. They will help to smooth the tail hair down as well as protecting the tail while the horse is travelling to the competition.

Polo wraps are made from strong, shock-absorbent felt. Unlike traditional bandages, polo wraps do not require padding underneath.

A **cohesive bandage** is a stretchy bandage which sticks to itself. It can be used as an alternative to an exercise bandage or for holding dressings and poultices in place.

PADS

Bandages should never be applied directly to the leg (except for polo bandages) but should be used with bandage pads to help reduce the risk of pressure sores developing on the legs.

Felt pads are hardwearing and shock absorbent, but they do not mould easily to the shape of the horse's leg. **Cotton quilted pads** are easily washable and hardwearing but, like felt, do not mould easily to the horse's leg. **Porter boots** are hard-shelled leg protectors which mould to the shape of the horse's leg and are held in place with an exercise bandage. They are used instead of pads to protect the leg from injury during competitions.

▮ LEFT
travelling or stable
bandages

▮ BELOW LEFT
exercise or tail bandage

▮ BELOW RIGHT
polo wraps

▮ ABOVE LEFT
stable bandages

▮ ABOVE RIGHT
Porter protector

▮ LEFT
cohesive bandage

PUTTING ON AN EXERCISE BANDAGE

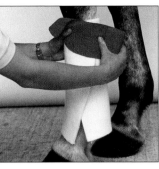

EXERCISE BANDAGES

Exercise bandages and polo wraps are used to protect the horse's legs during exercise or work. A great deal of skill is required to apply bandages which are neither too tight (which can lead to damaged tendons), nor too loose (when they can unravel and cause the horse to fall). Exercise bandages must always be applied over some sort of padding, such as a Gamgee, Fybagee or Porter boot.

1 Place the padding around the leg, making sure that the edge of the pad lies between the tendons, on the outside of the leg. The padding should start just below the knee or hock and finish just below the fetlock joint. Wrap the pad around the leg firmly, from front to back, making sure that there are no lumps or wrinkles.

2 Bandage in the same direction as the padding and start just below the padding at the top.

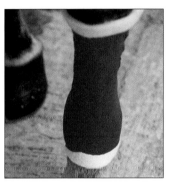

3 Do one complete turn with the bandage around the top of the padding before working down the leg. Exercise bandages are elasticated so be careful not to pull the bandage in too tightly.

4 Make sure that the bandage stays smooth and that the tension is even.

5 At the bottom of the leg the bandage should follow the same angle as the fetlock joint so that it forms a V at the front of the leg. This will ensure that the movement of the fetlock is not restricted.

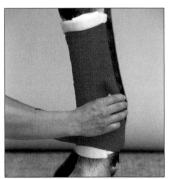

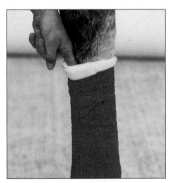

6 Continue to wrap the bandage around the leg, working back up to the top of the padding.

7 Secure the bandage by fastening the ties with a simple knot. The knot should be flat and sit on the outside of the leg. For competitions, stitch the bandage to ensure that it stays in place. Cover the stitched end with insulating tape.

8 The bandage should be firm enough not to slide down but not so tight that it could damage the tendons. You should just be able to slide your finger inside the bandage.

Travelling Equipment

▮ RIGHT
padded tail guard

Special clothing can be used to protect the horse from injuries incurred during transportation in a horse truck or trailer.

A **tail guard** prevents the horse from rubbing his tail when travelling. Linen and cotton tail guards are secured with strips tied to the surcingle. The padded tail guard is fitted with Velcro fastenings.

Shaped travel boots can be used instead of travelling bandages to protect the front and hindlegs, from the coronet up to the knee and hock. **Travel boots** are simple square wraps which give protection to the lower leg.

Hock boots, made from leather and felt, are fitted over the top of travel bandages to protect the hock from injury, in the same way that **knee pads** are used to protect the knees. **Felt travel pads** under travel bandages will do the same job.

A **poll guard**, made from leather with a felt lining, provides protection for the sensitive poll area of the horse's head. It is attached to the headcollar or halter.

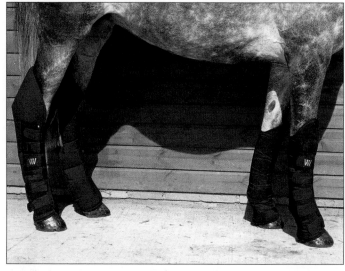

Shaped travel boots. These are designed for front or hindlegs to protect them from the coronet right up to the knee or hock.

Travel boots. These simple square padded wraps are effective in protecting the lower leg.

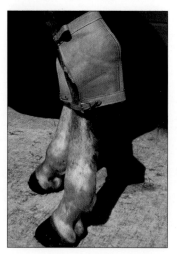

Hock boots. These are fitted to protect the hock joint from injury during transit.

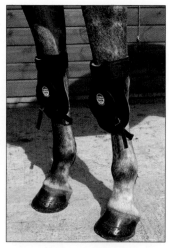

Knee pads. These can be used with travel bandages to protect the knees from damage.

HORSE DRESSED FOR TRAVELLING

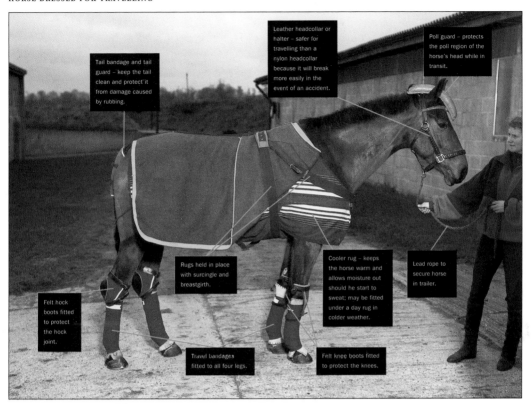

Tail bandage and tail guard – keep the tail clean and protect it from damage caused by rubbing.

Leather headcollar or halter – safer for travelling than a nylon headcollar because it will break more easily in the event of an accident.

Poll guard – protects the poll region of the horse's head while in transit.

Rugs held in place with surcingle and breastgirth.

Cooler rug – keeps the horse warm and allows moisture out should he start to sweat; may be fitted under a day rug in colder weather.

Lead rope to secure horse in trailer.

Felt hock boots fitted to protect the hock joint.

Travel bandages fitted to all four legs.

Felt knee boots fitted to protect the knees.

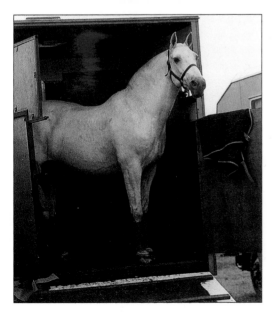

❚ LEFT
Horses are very vulnerable to minor injuries when travelling on the roads. While a complete set of travelling equipment is not always necessary, your horse should be fitted with leg protection and a rug. Regular safety checks should also be made on the trailer itself.

Shaped travel pads can be used in conjunction with travel bandages to protect specific parts of the legs when the horse is in transit.

Corrective Equipment

The following pieces of equipment may be used on the horse to discourage or prevent bad habits when he is stabled or turned out to grass.

A **plastic muzzle** may be used on a horse who is on a strict diet but needs to be turned out. The muzzle prevents him from eating large amounts of food, while the holes in the design allow him to breathe and drink. Plastic muzzles are also useful for horses who bite, chew their rugs or eat their bedding. The design of the **leather muzzle**, made of thick strips, allows the horse to breathe and drink but, like the plastic muzzle, it prevents him from nibbling his rug and biting.

A **bib** is attached to the headcollar and sits below the horse's chin. Like the muzzle, it is fitted to prevent the horse from chewing his rugs or bandages. A much more restrictive item is the **neck cradle**, which should be used only as a last resort to stop a horse from chewing.

A **cribbing collar** is a strong leather strap which is fitted tightly around the horse's throat to prevent him from crib biting and wind-sucking. The collar will not cure the condition, but will stop him doing it while it is fitted.

The design of the leather muzzle allows the horse to breathe and drink but will not allow him to bite and chew.

A plastic muzzle may be used on a horse on a diet who nonetheless needs to be turned out.

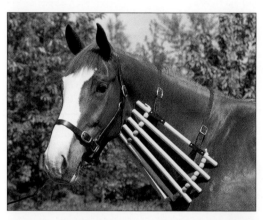

▌ LEFT
The neck cradle offers a last ditch attempt to stop a horse chewing rugs or bandages.

Cribbing collar. This is fitted around the horse's throat to prevent crib biting and wind-sucking.

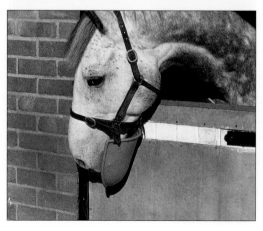

▌ LEFT
The plastic bib is a mildly restrictive piece of equipment which will help to dissuade the horse from chewing his clothing.

Grooming Equipment

Regular grooming is an essential part of good horse management. Besides making the horse look smart, it will help to keep him healthy. By removing accumulated dust, dead skin and hair, the pores of his skin are kept open, and the system for the regulation of body temperature – sweating – is able to function properly. While the stabled horse needs daily grooming, both before and after exercise, the grass-kept horse requires far less attention.

Brushing the horse cleans his coat, and will serve as a massage to improve muscle tone and circulation. The **dandy brush** has long, stiff bristles for removing dried mud or sweat from grass-kept horses, but it can be harsh on finer-coated stabled horses and should be used only on their legs. The **cactus cloth** is ideal for loosening dirt from areas too sensitive for a dandy brush.

The **body brush** has short, fine bristles designed to remove dirt and dead skin from the horse's coat. Use the brush in conjunction with a **metal curry comb**: draw it across the metal curry comb every two or three strokes to remove dirt and grease. The body brush will remove the natural oils from the horse's coat – oils which help to maintain the water-repelling properties of the coat – and is not recommended for horses who live out.

A **face brush** is smaller than a body brush and has softer bristles, making it ideal for grooming the horse's head.

The **water brush** has softer bristles than a dandy brush. Use it to dampen down an unruly mane and tail, and for washing muddy hooves.

■ **ABOVE**
Dandy brushes with synthetic bristles (*left*) and natural bristles are ideal for field-kept horses.

■ **LEFT**
Synthetic (*far left*) and leather body (*left*) brushes. These should only be used on stabled horses.

■ **LEFT**
metal curry comb

■ **BELOW**
A water brush can be used to dampen the horse's mane and tail.

■ **BELOW**
Plastic curry combs, including one with a hose attachment (*left*).

■ **BELOW**
rubber curry comb

■ **BELOW**
A rubber washing mitt will have a pleasant massaging effect on the horse's skin.

■ **RIGHT**
A face brush is a small soft brush used to groom the horse's head.

■ RIGHT AND
BELOW
trimming (*right*) and
thinning scissors (*below*)

A **plastic curry comb** will remove dried mud from the horse's coat, but take care when using it on very sensitive or ticklish horses. Some combs can be fixed to a hose for washing down dirty or sweaty horses. The softer **rubber curry comb** is used in a circular motion to remove dried mud and loose hairs, and to massage the horse's skin.

Drawing a **rubber washing mitt** over the horse's body when washing him will have a massaging effect as well as helping to remove dirt and sweat from his coat. A **sweat scraper** can be drawn across the horse's body, following the lie of the coat, to remove excess water after washing.

A **massage pad**, made from padded bridle leather, can be used to rub the neck, shoulders and hindquarters to improve tone and circulation. To give the coat a final polish after grooming, dampen a **stable rubber**, which is a cotton cloth or terry towel, and draw it over the horse following the lie of the coat.

The **hoof pick** is used to remove mud, stones and soiled bedding from the feet; a folding version can be safely carried in a pocket for use on rides. The **hoof-oil brush** is used to apply hoof-oil or dressing to the horse's feet, to stop them drying out and becoming cracked.

Every grooming kit should contain two **sponges**, one for cleaning the eyes and nostrils and one for cleaning the dock.

■ BELOW
Plaiting tubes are small rigid tubes used to hold mane plaits in place.

A **mane comb** is used to remove knots from the mane before plaiting (braiding). Use a **pulling comb** to pull manes and tails. The **Solo mane comb** trims and thins the mane without pulling out the hairs.

Mane thinning scissors have grooved blades and will thin the mane for a smarter appearance. **Trimming scissors** have curved blades to prevent accidental injury to the horse. Use them to trim the fetlocks and heels, as well as the bridle path (the part on the horse's crest where the headpiece of the bridle sits).

Use **quarter markers** to produce smart patterns on the hindquarters. Lay a plastic sheet over the hindquarter and draw a body brush over the top to produce an attractive pattern on the horse's coat.

The traditional method of fixing mane and tail plaits (braids) for shows and competitions is with a **plaiting needle** and **thread**, but elasticated **plaiting bands** are also available. Sewn plaits require more skill than bands but the finished look is smarter. Easy-to-use **plaiting tubes** are often used on dressage horses.

■ LEFT
Mane combs (*far left*), plaiting bands (*centre*) and a pulling comb (*below*).

■ BELOW
A sponge and a sweat scraper are used when bathing horses.

▮ RIGHT
Use a body brush to groom a stable-kept horse. Used with a metal curry comb it will effectively remove dirt and grease from the horse's coat.

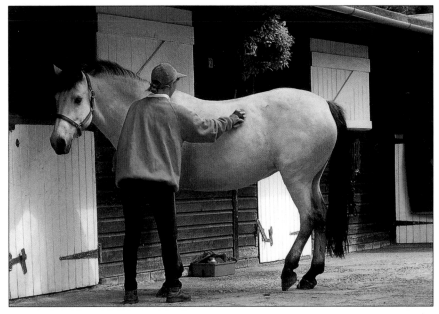

▮ BELOW
Plaiting (braiding) needle and thread. This is the traditional method of fixing mane and tail plaits.

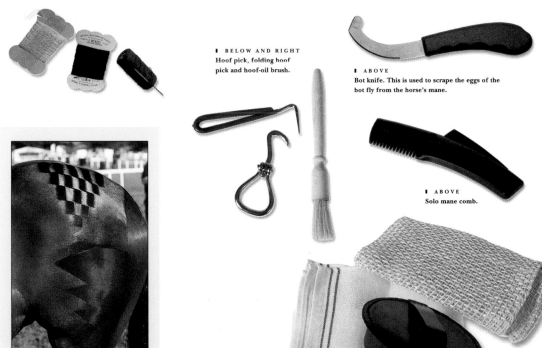

▮ BELOW AND RIGHT
Hoof pick, folding hoof pick and hoof-oil brush.

▮ ABOVE
Bot knife. This is used to scrape the eggs of the bot fly from the horse's mane.

▮ ABOVE
Solo mane comb.

Use quarter markers for a professional look that will add the finishing touch to a well turned out show horse or pony.

▮ RIGHT
Cactus cloth, stable rubber (rub rag) and leather massage pad.

Suppliers

The author and publishers would like to thank the following companies for supplying the tack and equipment featured in this book:

UNITED KINGDOM

Aerborn Equestrian Ltd
Pegasus House
198 Sneiton Dale
Nottingham NG2 4HJ

Albion Saddlemakers Co Ltd
Albion House
55 Caldmore Road
Walsall
West Midlands WS1 3NA

Clyst Equestrian Ltd
Teko House
Furnham Road
Chard
Somerset TA20 1AX

Keenthorne Saddlery
Nether Stowey
Bridgwater
Somerset

Miller Crosby Ltd
30 Birchbrook Industrial Estate
Shenstone
Nr Lichfield
Staffordshire WS14 0DT

Proteq™ Worldwide Ltd
Graingers
West Ashling
Chichester
West Sussex PO18 8DN

The Royal Mews
Buckingham Palace
London SW1W

Shires Equestrian Products
15 Southern Avenue
Leominster
Herefordshire HR6 0QF

Stylo Matchmakers International Ltd
Holybrook Mill
Harrogate Road
Greengates
Bradford
West Yorkshire BD10 0QW

Wychanger Barton Saddlery
The Haywain
Burlescombe
Nr Tiverton
Devon EX16 7JY

UNITED STATES

Whitman Saddle Manufacturing
5272 West Michigan
Kalamazoo
MI 49006

Libertyville Saddle Shop Inc.
P.O. Box M
Libertyville
IL 60048-4913

Fennell's Horse Supplies
Red Mile Road
Lexington
KY 40504

Drury's Saddlery and Supplies
1638 Danville Road
Harrodsburg
KY 40330

We are also grateful to the following for allowing their equipment, horses and stables to be photographed:

Betty Howett
Bossington Stables
Bossington
Nr Minehead
Somerset

Mrs Mary King
School House
Salcombe Regis
Devon EX10 OJQ

Bob Mayhew
Dumpford Manor Farm
Trotton
Hampshire GU31 5JR

Lynn Russell
Durfold Farm
Plaistow Road
Surrey EV8 4PQ

Sarah Rowe
4 Cleal Cottages
Broadway
Ilminster
Somerset TA19 9RD

Margaret Swords
White Horse Lodge
Over Stowey
Bridgwater
Somerset

Hannah Washer
Fulbrook Cottage
Fiddington
Nr Bridgwater
Somerset

Megan Williams
The Moat House
Longdon
Nr Tewkesbury
Gloucestershire